I Shoulda Been Home Yesterday

David Harris

I shoulda been home yesterday

DELACORTE PRESS / SEYMOUR LAWRENCE

365.6.092   Hz4n

c-1 APR 7 '77

Manufactured in the United States of America

First printing

Library of Congress Cataloging in Publication Data

Harris, David, 1946–
  I shoulda been home yesterday.

  Autobiographical.
  1. Harris, David, 1946–   2. Prisoners—California
—Personal narratives. I. Title.
HV9475.C2H37 1976   365'.6'0924 [B]   76–7903
ISBN 0–440–04156–2

SE

AUTHOR'S NOTE

Because I had no one's permission to use their personal stories in this book, I have changed names and descriptions in an attempt to conceal their true identities; any actual resemblance is a mistake on my part. Although names and faces have been altered, the stories told are all true and, to my way of thinking, adequately represent the prison life I experienced and shared with thousands of others.

Part One

IN THE CUSTODY OF THE ATTORNEY GENERAL

July 1969–August 1969

Harris, David Victor

height: 6'2''
weight: 165 lbs.
hair: blond
eyes: blue
scars, marks: 2'' left knee
birthdate: 2-28-46
sentence: Federal, 3 years
         refusal subm.
         induct.
assignment: A-3

1

The first cop I ever met was in Fresno, California, where I grew up. Fresno was a skinny town then, and greasy. All the people I knew who had any money worked for it, but the town was big enough so that I didn't know all that many people when I was twelve and they weren't.

I was at Uncle Elmo's when I made the acquaintance of the police. Elmo was my great-uncle and had what was called a ranch out past Clovis. What it really was, was two houses, a chicken coop, six goats, a cow, and an Indian woman. The Indian woman was forty years younger than Uncle Elmo and was there to make sure Uncle Elmo didn't fall down the stairs and break a leg. He never did. So Grandma liked the Indian woman. She especially liked Uncle Elmo. He lived off her, a little money he'd saved from his job at the planing mill, and a government check. My grandma would take me out to see him and to do a little work. I used to nail up the chicken coop, watch the Indian woman, and chase Elmo's cow around the back part of his ranch, near the county land.

It was winter then. Fog was laid up on the side of everything that didn't move and half the things that did. In the winter, the sheriff ran a work camp not far from Elmo's. The prisoners cut firewood for the summer campgrounds by the lake. I was out chasing Elmo's cow and walked into the sheriff's camp.

There was a lean-to on top of a stubby rise, and stacks of wood all over. A man in a brown uniform swallowed the doorframe of the shack. I walked up to him.

"Seen a cow with brown spots?" I asked.

"No," he said. "That what brought you over on the county land?"

I nodded.

"Well, watch your step," he warned. "This is the sheriff's camp, and them's county prisoners and I'm responsible for em. Deputy Griswold's the name."

I was impressed.

Deputy Griswold noticed I was impressed, so he invited me into his shack. "Come on in here," he said, "it's warm and I'll give ya a cup of coffee."

I went inside and it was warm. A potbellied stove squatted in the corner with a coffeepot on its beak. The shack was bare boards except for the spots where Deputy Griswold had pasted decorations on the wall. One was a newspaper clipping about a hatchet murder six years earlier in Salinas. The rest were pictures of naked women.

All of the women had enormous breasts with nipples that hung out like erasers off the ends of brand-new pencils. The biggest picture was of a blonde who had a Coke bottle clenched between her knees.

The deputy saw me looking at the woman and her tits and the Coke bottle. "That's a hell of a picture ain't it?"

"Sure is," I said. It was. Sometimes I still remember it.

"Got it four years ago down in Pinedale. A friend of mine runs a bar there and sells me pictures. Says he knows the broad himself, but I don't believe it. Shit, he ain't but five foot three, and that kinda woman'd laugh him outta the sack." The deputy laughed a laugh like a gobbler.

"I guess so," I said.

I was sitting in the only chair. The deputy was sitting on a crate. He was a wide man. With his feet up on the stove, Griswold took up half the shack. Except for his head. He had a small head. Much too small for his shoulders and his great stubby neck. Deputy Griswold's head balanced up there like a grape.

"What you do out here?" I asked after we'd sipped from our cups for a while.

"My prisoners cut wood and I watch em," Deputy Griswold answered.

"Don't they run away?" I asked.

"No, they don't." The deputy's mouth crept around his face so he talked out of the side of his head, all of the time watching the pictures on the wall, like they might jump off and run for the door. "I got em trained," he explained.

The deputy had tiny holes running up and down his face in herds. "Once," he continued, "one of em jumped me with a pitchfork and put a hole in my shoulder, but I knocked him down and kicked his nuts up to the roof of his mouth. Never had no more trouble." The deputy turned to a prisoner who'd come in the door. "Ain't that right?"

The prisoner wore a denim coat and pants. He was an old wino with skin that hung like wet laundry on his face.

"Sure is, boss," he said.

The old wino was standing in front of the blonde's picture.

"Say, old wino," the deputy offered, "why don't you move your ass over a coupla steps, you're blocking the view."

The old wino cringed, said, "Yessir, boss," and the picture blared out like a blister on the wall.

I was impressed.

The deputy saw I was impressed and offered me another cup of coffee. I didn't take it. I'd hardly touched the one I had, and Grandma didn't like me to drink coffee. Besides, I had to leave and find the goddamn cow.

When I finally found it, the cow was down by the marsh. I took the road back to Elmo's ranch. It was almost dark by the time I got back. The sheriff's bus passed me on the way. The deputy had his grape head bunched up over the wheel, and everyone else looked to be asleep.

Grandma was waiting at Uncle Elmo's. She was sitting on the porch. Uncle Elmo hadn't fallen down the steps while I was gone. Grandma had seen to that while the Indian woman made biscuits. We ate the biscuits, then drove back to Fresno. I forgot Deputy Griswold before we were halfway home.

At the time, I thought the law was something people did to give old winos a little exercise in the fresh air.

When I was older and on my own, I learned better.

2

On my way toward twenty-one, the law and I headed in different directions. The way I look at it, I didn't change course at all. It's the law that got lost.

I grew up believing in high school civics and never did lose my faith. What changed was the tense of it all. I once thought all the stuff the eleventh-grade teacher talked about was what we *had*. Almost as soon as I left Fresno, I began to feel like it was an arrangement we needed to *get*. The first lesson I learned in that direction was taught by the sovereign state of Mississippi, nineteen hundred and sixty-four.

Five of us had driven there nonstop after a rally at Stanford in late September. I was eighteen years old and looking for something to stand up for. The right of black people to vote was just the kind of cause I had in mind. A guy named Frank and I were sent by SNCC to Quitman County in the delta, and told to find the Freedom House in a town called Marks. We did. The house was the second floor of a lodge hall on the niggers' side of town. Paint was falling off the walls so that the building looked like a half-peeled fruit. We fit right in. To the white folks we were a sort of nigger, too. Some weird kind they grew out in California.

In fact, I was young and scared and getting my education real quick. Over the next two weeks I was spat upon, threatened with knives and guns, and run out of two of the county's surrounding towns. Two days before we arrived, the local sheriff arrested a seventy-four-year-old black woman for trying to register to vote, and stuck a cattle prod into her vagina. When Frank got jumped and beaten one night on his way to the mailbox, the sheriff declined to investigate at first. It wasn't until the FBI got involved that his hand was forced.

The FBI got called in because Frank was from California and his girl friend's daddy was president of a university. Two agents came by to investigate on a Saturday morning, and knocked on the downstairs door. I answered after checking them out from the second-floor window. The chill that had been seeping around the door hit me in the face when I opened it The first agent flashed his badge.

"Federal Bureau of Investigation," he said.

I smiled. At that point, I figured the two things on a civil rights worker's side were the reporters and the FBI. That impression lasted another fifteen seconds while the agent looked up from my feet to my work-shirt. When his dark glasses reached my face, he spoke with the sound of the men who lived on the other side of town.

"Well, nigger-lover," he said. "What seems to be the problem?"

From then on, I figured I didn't have nearly as much on my side as I once believed. When the sheriff called me on the phone and said I ought to come down to the jail and turn myself in for beating poor Frank like I had, I didn't think twice. Frank and I left Quitman County an hour later, crossed into Louisiana the same day, and headed straight through to California, stopping only for gas.

By the time we reached Needles, 1,500 miles away,

I'd decided that my future wasn't going to be exactly as I'd planned. High school civics had turned out to be something that could get someone in a lot of trouble. One of those someones was me.

It was dark around Frank's 80-mile-an-hour car and the desert was falling on either side like the wake of a ship.

3

Two years later, my feelings began to come true.

The problem was named Vietnam and it got burned into the hide of my life. From the first thing I heard about the war, it smelled bad. Thousands of folks were dying in the worst way for the sake of fat generals, John Wayne movies, and South Asian rip-off artists who learned about elections from the CIA. I looked over my notes from high school and the situation didn't resemble a thing I'd been taught. I was twenty years old and the first president of the Stanford Student Body in years to have hair on his face. I was intent on making my mark on the world and figured to do it for the best thing I knew. Not killing people for the wrong reason was the principle I chose. I wasn't going to soldier in this one.

The first thing I did was send a letter to my draft

board with my student deferment card enclosed. I told them that if people were going to be forced to run that meat-grinder it shouldn't be just those who couldn't afford to go to college. I got no answer.

Two months later, I sent another letter and enclosed the rest of my Selective Service identification. I told them I was just one person but I wasn't a tool to be used for that kind of business. I said they wouldn't get any more cooperation from me. I swore I'd find more just like myself and teach the government that if it was going to shred Indochina it would have to do so without any draftees. They didn't answer, but I tried hard to live up to my promise anyway.

By October 16, 1967, a group of four of us called the Resistance had grown to 4,000 and all of us had sent our draft cards back. In November, we returned 1,500 more. In the meantime, my draft board lost its patience and ordered me to report to the Oakland Induction Center on January 17, 1968. I got as far as the front door and turned around.

When the Honorable Oliver Carter Presiding pronounced sentence on May 28, 1968, he called it a willing "refusal to submit to a lawful order of induction." The jury on my case had been out eight hours before he'd instructed them that the only possible verdict was guilty. It was nine o'clock at night. Except for my trial, the Federal Building was closed. Noise in the halls echoed all around the seventeenth floor. Carter sat over everyone's head behind a mound of walnut and in front of a bronze eagle with a six-foot wing span. I was standing while he sat and read.

"You," he said with a long pause, "have been found guilty by a jury of your peers." Carter paused again, chewing a sentence between his teeth. "Normally," he continued, "sentence is a question of rehabilitation. Your case is an exception. You don't need to be re-habilitated. You don't want to be rehabilitated. Perhaps you shouldn't be rehabilitated. But you will be punished." After that came the part about three years in the custody of the Attorney General, and Judge Oliver Carter Presiding left the room. He said I could appeal the verdict if I wanted to.

I did, but lost that one, too. The time was rapidly approaching when the law and I would meet head-on.

4

It was July 15, 1969. Two federal marshals came to my house with a warrant. They came in a Dodge and two sharkskin suits. They also came in sirens, badges, and nickle-plated handcuffs. I'd seen them before. They came to our demonstrations. They came to my trial. This time they brought a paper along that said I was their property right then and there. "In the custody of the Attorney General" is what the judge called it. From then on, I began to see the law in a brand-new way.

The marshals' suits sweated in the sun. Some kind of thin, invisible cosmic grease.

"You Harris?" they asked. They were in the door.

So was Joanie. She was my wife, and looked like

she'd swallowed a small watermelon. It came from being pregnant.

"Among other things," she said.

"Not you," they said.

"You don't like me," she said.

"Nothin personal, ma'am," the first marshal answered, "but we're after your husband, there." I was three steps behind her. The marshal and his sharkskin suit both pointed at me.

We all stood still. I stood in the kitchen and Joanie and the first marshal and the second marshal and her stomach all stood in the doorway. We stood still until the second marshal began to scuff his feet.

"Come on," he said.

I did, and the marshals relaxed a little. When we got outside where they could see their Dodge, the first one offered to let me say good-by to my wife.

"Looks like I'm gonna be gone for a while," I said.

"It sure does," she said.

"I guess I'll catch you later," I said. I was running out of words and feeling my future breathing down my neck.

"Good-by," she answered.

I watched her over my shoulder as the marshals and I walked off.

Then we drove away. The marshals, the Dodge, the sirens, the badges, the handcuffs, and me. Joanie and her stomach stayed behind, along the side of the road. After the first curve, I couldn't see them at all.

5

I lived in the Santa Cruz mountains south of San Francisco then, and getting from there to jail was a downhill ride. The Dodge started to wallow through a hundred and seventeen curves and cutbacks on our way to the flatlands. It wasn't the kind of road you want to drive a Dodge on. The front end was sloppy, and the ass end a roller coaster. I was in the back seat, with the handcuffs and the siren. I was chained to my waist and I bounced. First to one side and then back to the other.

The marshals were in the front seat, talking about their suits and their work around the office. They got their suits at Roos Atkins. The first marshal also got a smuggler once in the stomach as he ran out a door.

They talked about it until I interrupted them halfway down the hill. I spoke to the second marshal, the one who wasn't driving.

"Say, Marshal," I said. He swiveled his head. "Where'd you say you got those suits of yours?"

"What's it to you?" he said back.

"Well," I explained, "I was gonna suggest you order another one. You got me all chained up here so all I can do is bounce from door to door. That bouncin has made me sick. Much more of it and my breakfast and your suit are gonna be the same thing."

"You sick?" he said.

"I'm sick," I said.

He rolled his window down. "Is that better?" he asked.

"No," I answered, "it sure isn't."

We stopped on a loop of road overlooking the slope. The second marshal opened my door. I doubled up in my handcuffs and puked. The vomit splattered on my boots and dripped off my chin. Down to my left was the freeway. Traffic was moving steady, the way late-morning traffic always does. The diesels gearing down from the rise made sounds like a long hallway of doors slamming, one by one.

It was a sound I got used to. The noise was the anthem of my life for the next twenty months. It was during that time, when I was owned by it, that I got to know the law the way I do. The first thing I learned is that the Attorney General and his friends do whatever they please with the lives the judge sends their way.

6

I learned that much just listening to Crazy Leon.

Crazy Leon had a lot of problems. The biggest one was that he was crazy. I mean righteously crazy. He thought he was a wolf and did all the things wolves do. At night, he howled. Just like a goddamn wolf: "Oooowoooooooooooooooowoooooo."

Crazy Leon was one of my neighbors. He lived two doors down in an isolation cell and I grew to hate him. Night after night, I woke to the sounds of a nearby wolf hankering after a concrete moon.

Leon's cell was five feet wide and seven feet high. It had a peekhole in the solid door and a shithole in the floor. No windows. The shitter had a grate on it with two crescent shapes along the edges and a circle in the middle. If his aim was off, Leon had to poke the turds through the grate with his fingers, and they sat for a day or two while the cop in the hallway decided whether or not it was time to flush the shithole. Leon was considered too dangerous to be given a toilet he could flush himself.

Or a light switch. His little world was lit by 150 watts screwed into the ceiling and covered with mesh. Crazy Leon never howled when the light in his cell was on. He'd just sit in his underwear, curled up in a corner. When the lights went off at ten o'clock, Leon's wolf job commenced: "Oooowooooooo . . . oowoowoowooooooo."

Leon kept at it until the deputy came down the hall and kicked on his door. "Shut up, you crazy son of a bitch," the deputy ordered.

"Groooof," Leon barked back.

The rest of us heard Leon's growl gear down into a yap, and then we heard the deputy getting his keys. All the while, Leon was holding a low, long whine that crawled up the cop's pants and made his leg hairs stand on end.

"Rrrrrr," Leon snarled.

Then the cop hit him. Right across the face with a little six-inch wooden club with lead filling in the end. I heard the deputy hit Leon again, and twice more after that until Leon stopped his whine. He stopped yipping and growling too. The cop closed the door and the rest of the cell block went back to sleep.

The morning shift opened Leon's cell as soon as breakfast was over. First, they turned on the light. Then they put him in the middle of a bed sheet and dragged him to the shower. The morning shift washed the clotted blood off Leon as best they could.

When Leon was clean and starting to come to, the cops walked him down the hallway past the cell I shared with seven others. He made a few whimpers that crawled up the walls like insects.

7

The walls were two feet thick and reinforced concrete. As buildings go, this one wasn't likely to fall down, and it would be hard for a man with a sharp spoon to burrow his way out. Nobody did while I was there. Instead, we called the place names. Some of us called it the slam, some of us called it county jail, some of us called it motherfucker. I called it the Zoo.

All the names fit.

Inside those walls, up on the seventh floor, there were twelve long rows of cages, each one too small to park a car in and each one full of piss smells and body hair. Each one so full of men there was just enough room to sleep and wake up. To get to those cages, I went through the underground garage first.

The marshals' Dodge parked in a cavern lit by long, straight lines of fluorescent tubes, and full of police cars. The marshals guided me, one attached to each arm.

"Watch your step," the first marshal said when we got to the elevator.

The door opened after he pushed the button, but he first unlocked a small steel drawer next to it. Then he pulled his .38. It was chrome-plated. He rubbed the gun with his handkerchief before putting it in the drawer. The second marshal did the same, and we got in the elevator.

Our first stop was the third floor. The marshals and I got out into the long, straight light and went up to a counter. It was then that I first noticed the air. The air seemed to lie on the back of my neck like it was alive.

All the air in the Zoo came from metal ceiling grates. At least that's where it came out. Nobody knew where it came from. My guess was a big fan on the roof sucked it in. By the time it reached the seventh floor, every stray fart in the neighborhood was riding on it. That's how you notice the air. It smells used. It's full of smoke, too. And it gets gummy so you have to breathe in patches. I learned to suck in through my mouth until I hit a pocket that hadn't been breathed but three or four times before. Then I'd swallow and look for more. After a while, you get to think of it as oxygen.

The marshals were fingerprinting me. Then they stacked my prints and stapled them to ten pieces of paper and gave the whole package to the secretary coiled up in back of the counter.

"One federal prisoner," the first marshal said.

She looked at me. "Sign here," she said to him.

The first marshal signed on the line. Then the second marshal signed and gave it to the secretary, who signed and gave it to the sergeant, who put it on his desk and signed a receipt. The secretary gave the receipt to the first marshal.

"One federal prisoner," she said.

We got back on the elevator. When the light lit at Number 5 the door opened and I saw a sign saying WOMEN'S WING. A woman got in with a cop. She had orange hair and shuffled along in her nylons and a skirt that stopped just short of the crack in her ass. The marshal pushed Number 7.

The woman looked at me. I looked back. I still had flakes of puke crusted on my shirt.

"You must be an awful bad man to be all chained up like that," she said.

"Oh, I am," I answered.

"What'd you do to be such a bad man?" The orange-haired woman cocked her head as she asked the question.

"I didn't kill anybody," I said.

"Oh," she said, "you are a bad man aren't you?"

The door opened at the seventh floor before I could pass on the rest of my biography. We all lined up at another counter. The orange-haired woman was first in line. The cop pulled her wig off when she reached the officer in charge. Under her wig, she had a crew cut.

"What's your name?" the sergeant behind the counter asked.

"George Lewis," the crew-cut woman answered.

The cop took George Lewis off through a locked gate and into the waiting cages.

The sergeant took my name and did the same with me. The marshals went back to the elevator, and I went with a deputy who sprayed flea powder on my body and sent me down to live next to Crazy Leon.

I never saw George Lewis again, but I heard she was up on the next block, sucking dicks in a cell by the barbershop.

8

As the deputy walked me toward my new home, I wasn't worried about it. That would come later when my circumstances had time to sink in. For those first few moments I was glad to be there. I was glad not to be waiting for it to happen. Whatever was ahead of me, I was about to begin doing it. When it was done, it would be behind me. It was a relief not to have to anticipate anymore. "Here I go," I said to myself.

What worries I did have centered mainly on my pants. The pair I'd been issued were four inches short in the leg and three inches too wide in the waist. To walk, I had to grab a handful of fabric, hold tight, and run the risk of going airborne in strong winds. When we left the clothing room, I asked the deputy about them.

"Do I have to share these," I said, "or take up all the slack by myself?"

"Keep that smart mouth," the deputy answered, "and I'll let you eat em for lunch."

I didn't say anything for the rest of the journey. I just flapped along in my denims until we reached A Block, Number 3 tank. That's where I lived for as long as I stayed in the Zoo.

Number 3 was six bunks, two mattresses on the floor, a sink, a shitter, a line of bars, eight men, a door, a lock on the door, and a whole lot of time.

9

Six of us in Number 3 had our sentences already, and were just waiting for a ride down the line to the penitentiary. We had thirty-four years to do among us. The other two had yet to get theirs, but one was facing five and the other anywhere up to thirty-five.

That was Uncle John facing the thirty-five. He'd been in Number 3 eight months waiting for his trial. When we first met, he said he'd probably be in court by September.

Uncle John was sure to be in Number 3 while he waited. Bail was a hundred thousand dollars and Uncle John, needless to say, didn't have it. Or at least he couldn't get to it. He said he had it, buried in the desert outside of Las Vegas. But Uncle John had stashed the map in a safe-deposit box that only his old lady could get into, and his old lady wasn't anywhere to be seen. The police wouldn't let her visit when she tried, and she hadn't written for six months. Uncle John missed her as much as the money. He said she was a fox.

And she was. I saw her when she finally came calling. You couldn't make out her eyes for the eyelashes, but you could see the rest of her and it was all good. The visit started with a letter Uncle John got in the Friday morning mail.

The mail comes through the bars right after the corn meal mush. The way the mush was, you could read it, eat the letter, and end up better fed. The mush just lay up on its steel dish and crusted over right before your eyes. If you were going to eat it, you had to eat quick. Big Al claimed the mush would glue your asshole shut if you ate it, but Machichi ate it all the time and it never did.

John put down his sheet of crinkly pink paper. "She's coming to visit," John said. Uncle John usually slept until at least ten, but here it was six o'clock in the morning, and there was John sitting up on his bunk like a bird on its perch. It was quiet. The only other sounds on the whole block were Machichi slurping his mush and someone grunting his way through a crap down in Number 1.

"She is?" I said.

"Yah," John raved from his top bunk. "Listen to this: 'Dear Butch . . .' She calls me Butch," Uncle John paused to explain. "'. . . I'm sorry I didn't write for so long. I've been in Houston and now I'm back. I called the jail and they said I could visit. I'm going to come and see you next Saturday. I can hardly wait to see you.

Love, Patti.' Did you hear that?" Uncle John exclaimed. "She can hardly wait to see me. Hot damn." Uncle John's face was all sucked up into his eyes. "She's comin tomorrow. Hot damn." Uncle John stayed awake all night waiting for the next day.

Uncle John was from Tracy, or at least that's where he started. He lived there until his mother died when he was fourteen. Then he knocked his father in the side of the head and took off. John ended up in Modesto, told a café owner he was seventeen, and was washing dishes until two hookers found him. These hookers adopted John, got him dressed down at Montgomery Ward, and sent him to school. He lived in the Travelers Hotel in a room right next to theirs for three years. During that time, John figured out what the ladies did until late in the night, and began to do a little of it himself. Uncle John became the youngest pimp in Modesto. Shortly after the beginning of his professional career, the hookers had to make a quick exit, and John was on his own again.

But now he had a trade, and practiced it for the next twenty-five years. Before he was busted, John was running all the pussy sold in Las Vegas. Or so he said. None of us knew for sure, but we believed him. Uncle John was a very believable guy. He showed me a picture of him and Lucky Luciano taken in Italy.

Uncle John was up on seven counts of the Mann Act: Interstate Transportation of a Person for Immoral Purposes. "It's such a goddamn mess," he explained. "This woman Shirley is talkin to the police. She used to be my old lady. I met her in Hayward and I brought her out to Vegas. When you got a string of women, one of em is always your old lady, and she keeps the rest in line. Shirley was a hell of an old lady, but then I met

Patti and I told Shirley she had to move down onto the string. She was pissed. Boy, let me tell you, she was pissed. Next day she just up and took off and I never heard nothin else about her for a year. Then I picked up a paper and I read that a trucker I used to know in Hayward had been shot. He used to sell these here fuck pictures on his truck route, and he was a punk. But this woman Shirley was arrested for it. Next thing I know, she'd given me up and the cops were on my ass. They caught up with me in L.A., kicked in the door of my motel room, and here I am."

Uncle John stopped to pick his nose. He used the first finger on his right hand, the one that had been cut off right above the knuckle.

"If I can just get bailed," he added, "I can get the shit together to beat the rap. I know I can." Uncle John said that over and over again as he waited through the night.

Saturday morning, the cops brought a razor by, and John shaved and went out to visit. He got his fifteen minutes up at the glass just like the rest of us, and came back to the tank.

"You watch," he told Big Al when the police finished locking the door behind him, "in another week I'll be out on bail and then you'll see my smoke. I'm gonna beat this motherfucker free and clear."

In a week, Uncle John still wasn't out on bail, but he did get another visit. Five minutes after his visit was called, he came back to Number 3. Packages of sweat and tears hung on his slowly crumbling face like balls on a Christmas tree.

"Shit," he said.

"What happened?"

"It's gone. All the money's gone."

"Who took it?"

"Nobody," he moaned. "It's still in the ground. But they built a suburb out there. It was just desert when I buried it two years ago. But my old lady went to dig it up and there was a Safeway on top of it."

Uncle John lay down on his belly, pulled the eight months he'd done and the thirty-five years he was facing over his head, and cried. The rest of us were being real quiet. There wasn't all that much else to do.

10

There wasn't a whole lot of space to do it in, either.

With everybody on his rack, Number 3 was eight men dangling their legs into a telephone booth. There was one space that wasn't covered by a body, and it was six feet long and two feet across. The open space started at the lip of the shitter and ended at the side of Machichi's bunk.

Big Al and Machichi used the space for push-ups. That was the stakes the two of them played hearts for. A push-up a point, and Machichi was always winning so Big Al was always getting exercise. He filled the opening with a crop of grunts that rose to the twenty-foot ceiling like bubbles in a fishbowl.

Not that Big Al needed to do push-ups. Big Al had

a pair of tree trunks growing out of his shoulders and he was famous for knowing how to use them. That is, Big Al was famous if you had ever been to the Slaughterhouse. It's a jail across the bay. Everybody over there had heard of him. He was a legend.

The Slaughterhouse is a concrete box two stories high and a block long. It's a hollow block. Inside, the cops walk a catwalk about twelve feet up the wall. From the catwalk, they can see into every one of the hundred and fourteen cells. The cells are five feet wide and seven feet high, with a solid door and no ceiling. Just cyclone wires strung where the ceiling was supposed to be, and a cop standing above the wire. Fire hoses are stationed all along the catwalks. That's one of the ways the police enforce their program. If the cops don't like what's happening in a cell, they just open the nozzle and bounce prisoners from wall to wall like a Ping-Pong ball.

The Slaughterhouse is laid out like a dead-end street. There's one corridor between the cells that runs into a wall at one end and into the police station at the other. Big Al used to get out in the hall once a week and walk to the shower and back. It was on Tuesday. Big Al would wait all week for Tuesday. He'd wait for the cop to pull his key, stick it in the door, and turn it. Then Big Al would come off the back wall like a dump truck. He'd kick the door into the cop's face, run down to the end of the hall, and get his back against the wall.

"Send me the police," he'd shout up at the catwalks. He said police with a long *o*, like a tunnel. "I got somethin I want to tell em."

Six police would be sent. Six police in visors and helmets, with long batons in their hands.

"Let me tell it to ya one at a time," Big Al would say. "I want to whisper it in your ear." Then he'd poleax the nearest cop and the game would start.

All told, it usually took fifteen minutes to get Big Al unconscious or at least pinned down. It took another five for the cops to figure out whether they'd hurt him enough. Then they'd throw him back in his cell and give Al the hoses for ten minutes. Right away, Big Al started waiting for the next Tuesday. Recreation is what he called it.

Finally Big Al finished his sixty days and left. It wasn't another month before he was across the bay in the Zoo, charged with possession of heroin. Folks from the Slaughterhouse would recognize Big Al when the cop walked our tank down the hall to the shower.

"Hey," they'd say, "will you look at that. The Zoo got that Joe Louis motherfucker too."

11

Number 3 got showered on Thursdays. Washing was one of five ways we could get out of the cell.

You could get a visit on Wednesdays or Saturdays.

You could go see the doctor on Tuesday mornings. The doctor was known as a wino. "Uppers or downers?" he'd ask, and give you two of your preference.

You could get one of the cops to give you a pass to

the barbershop if you arranged it ahead of time, and gave the barber four packs of Camels. The trusty would run them over to the next block and act as middleman in the deal.

Or you could go to church.

That's what Machichi, Big Al, and I did. We'd go to church every Sunday morning just so we could walk the forty-seven steps it takes to get from Number 3 to the chapel.

Those forty-seven steps cost us. We had to sit and not smoke for an hour while the minister preached and half of everybody else stood and sang hymns. They sang about the fortress of the Lord. We weren't into religion so we whispered a lot. But we weren't supposed to. We were supposed to be in church, and we all hid behind our hymnals. If the cop saw anything happening he didn't like, he'd jack the offender up and send him down to isolation. The cop sat inside a plastic bubble that lunged out from the wall. It was bulletproof, and he had a microphone, and he'd watch. If he called your name to the deputy by the door, you were on your way back thirty-nine steps to the cell next door to Crazy Leon's and just like his.

The minister stood behind a folding table with a cloth on it. A plaster cross stood like a hatrack in the corner. The minister was from the Salvation Army and he was Chinese. He wore a five-foot-three red-and-blue uniform, and talked about "Jesus Clist."

"Jesus Clist," he said, "has no melcy on those who do not confess and atone for their sins. . . . He is the son of a lighteous God who demands that He not be sinned against. . . . All sinners will be shown no melcy until you accept Him and His power. Those who sin without lepentance will burn in the Almighty God's wrath and justice. . . . Turn to page fifty-three and we shall sing."

Everybody stood up and bellowed like a herd of penned cattle.

The minister and his uniform talked on like that until eleven o'clock, when we were all marched out under the cop's turret and walked back to the tank.

The second Sunday I'd been there, Big Al and I noticed Machichi listening all through the service.

"Say, Professor," Machichi said after the cop locked us back up. He called me Professor because I wore glasses and had been to college. "Do you think we're all gonna roast like the Chinaman says?"

"I don't think people roast," I said.

"What about you, black man?" Machichi asked Big Al. "What you think?"

Big Al was lying back on his bottom bunk and had to lean forward to answer. "They can't send you to hell for shootin dope. Don't worry," he said, "that's all you and me has done cept for a little burglin, and that's all part of shootin dope."

12

That afternoon, Machichi told us about the most evil man he'd ever met. Talking like that was one of the things we did to pass the time.

"I'd been snatched on First Street and I had my fit

in my shoe," Machichi began. "The pigs didn't find no stuff cause if I had any I sure wouldn'ta been there in the first place. I was out on the pavement huntin. They put me up on a wall and found my homemade needle. So the cops put me in that new South County jail for, what you call it . . . paraphernalia? That's what they call havin a needle ain't it?"

There was light coming in from the afternoon outside the windows and lying all over Machichi's lap. The windows were on the other side of the bars on the opposite wall. The panes were frosted glass and locked shut so all we got from them was the light. No wind and no colors, but we dug it, just the thing for a Sunday after church. Because of the windows, A Block was a high-rent district, federal prisoners only.

"Sounds right," I said.

"In that place," Machichi continued, "everybody screams all day and it gets you crazy as a motherfucker. Eddie Hernandez and me got so crazy we threw our dinners in the cop's face. The bulls took us back to deadlock, where they keep you in a cell all day. There was six cells back there and they put me and Eddie in a cell together. On one side was a guy named Charlie and a *myati* dude that never said nothin. On the other side was this son of a bitch I was gonna tell tell you about.

"His name was Gringo, or at least Eddie started callin him that. This Gringo had a cell partner, an old guy, facin ten years for robbin a Gulf Station with a .45. This Gringo had manslaughter to do, which is anywhere up to fifteen, and he figured to do most of it. So Gringo says to his cell partner, 'Hey, cellie, why don't you and me bust outta this place?' Which ain't all that bad a idea to his cellie, who is mighty scared of those ten years he had sittin on him. So Gringo lays out his plan.

" 'It goes like this, cellie,' he says. 'The cop comes by here three times a day, right? He brings the food. That cop's key ring will get us all the way to the front door and I'll have my brother waitin in front. By the time they know we're gone, we're already on our way.'

" 'Sure,' his cellie says, 'but how are we gonna get the man's keys? I mean he ain't gonna give em to us is he?'

" 'It goes like this, cellie,' Gringo says. 'After he brings us dinner and he's still on the block, we pretend that you hung yourself and he's gotta open the door. When he does, I'll jump him, get his keys, and cut you down.'

"The cellie thought about it for a day before he said yes. He sent a note to his friend, Charlie, tellin him what he was gonna do, but Gringo didn't know that. Gringo just thought his cellie was thinkin it over. When his cellie said yes, this Gringo wanted to do it right away, but the cellie said they oughta wait a week. When the week was up, Gringo got his cellie up on a chair with a towel around his neck and the towel tied to a steam pipe.

" 'You gonna cut me down soon as you beat the cop, right?' the cellie said.

" 'Don't worry,' Gringo said.

"They both set their dinners on this Gringo's bunk, and Gringo pulled the chair out so his cellie just hung from the ceiling and swung back and forth. Then he sat down on the bunk and ate both dinners. After he ate, Gringo called the cop and told him his cellie had pulled his cork. Nothin was gonna happen, but Charlie finally told the cops about the note Gringo's cellie had sent him and Gringo got another manslaughter. He went on to Quentin and killed another cat. I think they're gonna gas him now."

After Machichi's story, things slowed down. In an hour, we were mostly watching the cracks in the ceiling and the flies in the hall. Machichi lay back and went to sleep in the thick light, snoring bricks.

I waited until it got dark to crash. When I did, I dreamed I was in a town square with burning telephone poles stuck in the ground. There was a platform in the middle of the square with a crowd of men at the top. I was standing at the dark edges, watching. A drum played. A man jumped off with a long rope tied around his neck. Just before the rope pulled tight, he shouted, "Freedom belongs to those who've lost it," and jerked straight out like a fish on a line. I woke up and looked across the bars until the picture passed from my mind.

13

It must have been late. The cell was dark except for the night lights. After ten, A Block was lit with weak blue bulbs, glowing like ripe plums in the ceiling. When I'd watched for a bit, Officer Furd came by with his flashlight. Officer Furd didn't start work until after midnight.

I began thinking about this lady I lived with for a

while. She had an apartment three blocks from Mickey's Blue Room and the Empire Café. This lady's place was on the third story and had an outside staircase. She had a scar that stretched like a suspender from the bottom of one of her tits down to her belly-button. When I started thinking about that lady, I grabbed the skin on my dick.

From then on, it was called the Prisoner's Shuffle.

Everybody's got to take care of himself, and whipping your pud is just one of the ways you can do it. I did it all the time, and it's not as simple as it sounds. You've got to do it with a certain respect for the neighborhood and an eye out for the police. If Officer Furd caught me working my meat, he would shine his light in my face, wake half the block, and ask if it felt real good or just average. Then he'd go back to the guard shack and tell stories about how he caught Harris whipping it. "Funniest thing I ever saw," he'd say. So I did it quiet. I bent my knees so the blanket draped over my body, faced the wall, and used a quick flip of the wrist that didn't shake the sheets too much. It's not like having a woman, but it does the job if assholes aren't your sport. It sure feels good when you get there too. I usually caught my wad in my shorts or in a puddle on my towel. Afterward, it was real easy to sleep.

I drifted off thinking about that lady with the scar. She had an apple tree in her yard, and smelled like apples. She smelled like every kind of apple there ever was.

Machichi was kicking his legs in his sleep.

I couldn't help but think it would be a long time before I got next to those apples again. A very long time indeed.

14

In Number 3 and all the rest like it, we told time with a calendar. We couldn't tell the hours apart and when the Zoo happened, it happened in days and weeks. If we measured our time in small chunks, there wasn't a whole lot to fill it with, and there sure was a lot of it to do. So most of us didn't mess with the date too much. We just let the month drag its ass across the concrete and gave it as little notice as pain would allow.

But sometimes it was just there and you couldn't stay away from it.

We were all sentenced. Our futures were occupied, and when you have the Attorney General sitting on your future, you learn just how big a thing a future can be. A man could break his back trying to hold it up. It's better to burrow into it and notice it as it's consumed.

15

Rufus's future caught up with him on August 5. That day, poor Rufus's future liked to kill him.

I'd been in the Zoo for three weeks then. In each of the weeks, folks would go to court and come back.

Others would be pulled out in the morning and taken off to whatever prison they were headed for. They just disappeared and nobody saw them again until we got down that line ourselves. Then you recognized a lot of old faces.

Rufus had been found guilty the week before, and on the fifth he went out in his court clothes to pick up his sentence. Three people from A Block went out for sentences that morning. They were Rufus and Gasmask from Number 4, and an Italian dude from Number 1. All of them were bank robbers. All of them had just been convicted for the first time. Rufus had pleaded guilty and so had the rest. Gasmask and the Italian were in front of Mount Rushmore, a San Francisco judge. Rufus was in front of a visiting judge from Delaware. Mount Rushmore gave the other two five a piece. The Delaware judge gave Rufus eighteen years.

"But, your Honor," Rufus's lawyer objected. He was a public defender with an office in the Federal Building, and had eighty-six cases to cover. "This is my client's first conviction. He has an excellent probation report. Couldn't that sentence be reduced to reflect the leniency and mercy of the court?"

"I would remind the counsel for the defense," the Delaware judge said, "the maximum sentence for bank robbery under federal law is twenty years. The court sentenced the defendant to eighteen. The court has been lenient and will tolerate no more discussion on the subject."

The public defender didn't say anything more. He just looked at the floor and then at Rufus.

"You'll tolerate it from me, you fat-assed son of a bitch," Rufus shouted. To make his speech, Rufus jumped up on the table. The bailiff and a marshal had him by the arms before he got two more words out, and dragged Rufus into the holding cell next to the courtroom.

Rufus was still talking about it when he and Gasmask were led back down the hall to Number 4.

"The court has been lenient, that motherfucker says. The court has been lenient. If he took them eighteen years he gave me, he couldn't talk that kinda shit," Rufus said.

Gasmask didn't say a thing.

But that didn't stop Rufus. He talked all through the rest of the morning. He talked through lunch too. Lunch was a plate of soup with a quarter-inch lid of grease on the top. The way we ate it was to break a hole in the grease with a spoon along the edge of the bowl, and slurp the liquid out.

Rufus talked on until Gasmask told him to shut up. "I'm sorry about your time and all, Rufus," he said, "but I can't listen to it no more."

Rufus threw his soup in Gasmask's face. Gasmask threw a fist back, and we began to hear crashing sounds right next door. When they were done, one of Gasmask's eyes was closed and Rufus's top lip was thick as his thumb. Rufus lay down on his bunk and went to sleep.

Everybody knew what had happened to Rufus and felt bad. The Zoo was close quarters, and one man's misery is infectious. It seeps from tank to tank.

In Number 3, Uncle John was thinking about his trial. I was thinking about the baby my wife was going to have. Machichi remembered San Jose. We all felt bad.

Big Al had gone to the barbershop.

16

When Al came back, he had something for our pain.

"Unstrap your arm," Big Al said, "we got a little pleasure comin up."

He produced a homemade hypodermic from his pants. From his shoe, he pulled a bag of Darvons. "Got the fit from the barber," he said. "I been scorin the rest from that wino on sick call."

It took Machichi fourteen seconds to roll up his sleeve and tie off his vein. The vein ran up the muscle of his arm like a rope. "Sweet," Machichi said, handing the outfit back, "real sweet."

The needle got to Texas last. He was the new man in our cell. He wasn't tied off yet when Uncle John shouted. Uncle John was the point man. He was up on the bars keeping watch for the police. "The Man is on his way," he shouted, and Texas stuffed the needle in his mattress.

The Man came right down to Number 3 and stopped. "Shakedown," the cop said as he opened the tank door. "Line up." He had three others with him, and in five minutes they had all of us stripped naked in the hall.

"Bend over and spread your cheeks," one of the cops told me. He had red hair and a nose like a doorknob. That's what all of us called him. Doorknob. I bent over and spread my cheeks. Doorknob looked in my asshole.

"You don't got no dope in there," Doorknob said with a laugh, "but it sure is a pretty asshole."

"Yah," I said between my legs, "paint a mustache on it and it'd look just like your mother." *(unsolitary)*

I spent the night down next to Crazy Leon for that one. Texas got the rest of the week there when they found the outfit in his mattress. All the noise woke Rufus up, and he started in again.

"Why don't you motherfuckers shut up," Rufus said to the deputies.

"Well, Rufus," the lead cop said, "we got our hands full now, but we'll be back for you later."

They came back on the midnight shift and grabbed Rufus when he was asleep. Officer Furd and Company took Rufus out in the hall and around the corner and beat him until he begged for his mama.

Rufus didn't talk much after that. In a week and a half, he was on his way to Leavenworth. I traveled with him as far as the eastern part of Arizona.

17

A lot happened before Rufus and I caught that bus. It all started the next day.

Uncle John got sick. He had a bad pair of lungs and they just seemed to get worse. Every time he thought of those thirty-five years, his chest cinched up and he gurgled like he was drinking a milk shake through a straw. Since the shakedown, Uncle John had picked up an abscess to go with the slop in his chest. He got the abscess from the needle that made its way around the cell. His arm was big as a watermelon, with a bump the size of a golf ball floating around the fresh needle hole. Uncle John was in bad shape.

He stayed that way all day. John lay on his bunk with his knees sucked up to his chest. Sometimes he moaned. Sometimes he slept. Sometimes he whined. "Did you hear that?" he'd say. His exhaling hit the walls like a wet sponge. "Oh, goddamn," he'd say. Uncle John got worse after dinner.

Dinner was a pile of noodles all stuck together with a vague meat paste. Nobody could be sure about the meat. Either it wasn't dead yet, or it had been dead for a very long time. Either way, it threatened to bite back, so the safest way to eat it was at arm's length. Machichi would throw a piece of Wonder Bread on it and smother the meat before it had a chance to strike. The rest of us usually passed on the noodles. "It's good stuff," Machichi'd say. "It'll kill your worms." I gave him mine every night. So did Big Al. For all the dinners we gave him, Machichi only puked it up once, so I guess it was all right. It was just looking at it that was hard.

After the trusty collected our plates and spoons, Uncle John set to moaning again. "Will you look at this," he said, and held up his arm. It looked like it might float away. "Oh, goddamn," he said. "I need some help."

"We got to call a cop," Big Al said.

So I called the cop by yelling through the front of the tank. "Officer," I called. "Officer, Officer." Nothing happened, so Big Al and I called him together.

When nothing happened again, everybody else in Number 3 joined in. Then we added our three tin cups on the bars and made a noise as big as the ones the dogs make at the pound.

That got results. The cop came running down the block. He was a baby cop. All the police do six months' probation before they're hired as regulars. The baby cop had just started his.

"What's the matter?" he asked.

"We got a sick man," I said. "He needs a doctor."

The baby cop looked at Uncle John. "I'll see what I can do," he said.

In half an hour, the lights were turned out right on schedule and the baby cop hadn't shown his face. The only light on the block was the blue bulb in the hall. We watched it for fifteen minutes and then made a noise bigger than anything the dogs at the pound ever dreamed of. Everybody in Number 3 was yelling except Uncle John. He'd done nothing except gasp for the last hour.

The first thing that happened put our noise to shame. A Block woke up and started screaming at us for our little two-bit clatter. As people found out why we were screaming, they screamed with us.

"There's a man dead sick in Number 3," Gasmask told Number 5, and Number 5 screamed like eighty mad bull apes. Penny Candy in Number 2 pulled the mattress off his steel bunk and beat that steel like he was all the tribes of Africa. One of the hippies in Number 1 recited the Declaration of Independence while banging on the bars with a steel cup. The forger who lived on the bunk next to Penny Candy blistered the paint on the wall with a yell that every buzzard in the state of California must have heard.

"Officer," Big Al chanted. "Officer, Officer. Officer. Officer." We let Big Al handle the bass line.

There was a kid in Number 1 with a brain tumor. His left eye wallowed out of focus most of the time, too. He stood on his bunk and began to list the Bill of Rights, banging on the ventilation shaft. It rang like a goddamn gong.

Then the second thing happened. The cop came back.

And he brought all his friends. The baby cop, Doorknob, the sergeant, the one we called Apeshit, and the one who had acne that spread all over his face and neck like napalm burns. They all came from our end of the hall. Five more gorillas I'd never seen before came in from the other end.

We stopped our noise. "There's a man sick," I said. "We told Junior there, but he didn't do nothin."

The sergeant looked at the baby cop. Then the five gorillas opened our door and carried Uncle John out. One on each leg and one on each arm. They took him out of the door at the far end. The rest of the cops huddled by Crazy Leon's cell.

After shuffling around, they all left except for the baby cop. He turned the lights on and walked down in front of our tank. Ours was the middle tank on the block. The baby cop opened his mouth and talked. "Because of the disruption you men created tonight, no one on this cell block will be allowed to have visitors for the next two months," he said.

We didn't say a thing back. We got real quiet and watched the baby cop, standing where everybody could see him. He had curly blond hair and lifted weights. When he'd watched us be quiet for a while, he walked down the block and turned the lights out.

The baby cop came by again in the dark. As he drew even with Number 3, Big Al spoke up. "You know what?" Al hissed. "If you were on my side of the bars, I'd wear your asshole on my finger like a ring."

The baby cop stopped dead in his tracks. "Who said that?" he yelled, staring into the black mass of our tank. By the time he switched his flashlight on, we were all asleep.

18

We were up with the mush the next morning. No visits for the two months was not something we could take lightly. We had one recourse. We talked to the marshals.

Everyone on our cell block was in the custody of the federal government, but we weren't yet in a federal institution. We were just on loan to the county hacks until we could be shipped off to the prison system. The marshals were responsible for us and had to come over to the jail every morning to check us out. If you had a need to talk, you just put in a request slip with the trusty who served the mush, and the marshal would have you brought up to the holding cells. We all put in slips.

A marshal with silver hair talked to me. "What's your problem?" he said.

"The cops here pulled our visits last night," I said. "Now we're federal prisoners, and it says right in the law books that we've got a right to visits. Most of us have people around here, and pretty soon we won't be nearly so close. The cops just took our visits because we called for help for a sick man."

"Well," the silver-haired marshal drawled, "you just stay calm and we'll see what we can do."

We waited for two days for the marshals to do something. The first of those days was a visiting day. None of us was allowed visits. The second day we saw the marshals again, and were told the same thing. Number 3 was pissed off.

"They ain't gonna do nothin," Machichi offered.

"Sure as shit they ain't," Texas said.

Pineapple had the bunk over Machichi's. "These motherfuckers never gonna do nothin," Pineapple chimed in. "So what can we do?"

"We can go on strike," I said.

"What're we gonna strike?" Texas asked. "We don't do nothin all day."

"I see you stuffin down all that slop they put in through them bars," Big Al interrupted. "You must be eatin when they ask you, cause I know you ain't eatin cause you like the food."

"We got to have some demands," Machichi added.

So we got a piece of paper and composed a document. "To whom it may concern," I wrote. "We, the inmates of A Block, will refuse to eat until the authorities meet the following demands:

1. Better medical attention. Give us a doctor every day.
2. Give us decent and nutritious food.
3. Give us some recreation and a TV set.

4. Return the visiting rights taken from us last Tuesday night."

"Sounds good," Big Al said.

When everybody had nodded their approval, Big Al got on the phone. Which is to say he walked up to the bars and shouted. "Hey," Big Al said, "we here in Number 3 got a proposal." Big Al proceeded to read our document. The reading was followed by a wide and flat mumble.

Slowly, folks returned Big Al's call.

"We're in," Rufus said for Number 4.

"So are we," Penny Candy replied. "We got a couple of whiners, but we'll kick em in the ass."

"Don't be talking that bullshit, Penny," another voice cut in, "we're all in."

"We want to think about it," Number 1 shouted. "We'll call back in the morning."

Big Al and I were worried whether Number 1 would come in. The bull moose in Number 1 was a mean son of a bitch called Snake. We didn't trust him because of what he did to the Fillmore Kid. The Fillmore Kid was one of Snake's crime partners, although Snake had started a long time before they met.

19

Snake's story started in the Atlanta penitentiary with Johnny, serving fifteen years for a bank robbery. He and Johnny still had to stand trial for another bank in Tennessee, and one day the marshals came to pick them up. They were supposed to drive to Memphis and get another fifteen years, but Snake stole a handcuff key. Before they were out of Georgia, Snake and Johnny jumped the marshals, handcuffed them to a tree, and drove their car to Knoxville. In Knoxville, they stole another car and robbed a gas station. Snake and Johnny didn't get much money from the station, but they were flush enough to make Indianapolis, where they robbed a bank. They robbed another in Kansas City, and two more in Colorado. At the one in Colorado Springs, Johnny shot a highway patrolman. The two fugitives made it to L.A. and robbed six more banks in the span of a month. They went to the Fillmore Kid's to hide out. Snake had known the Kid's father in the penitentiary.

"We're gonna rob a couple banks on the other side of the bay," Snake said. "But we need to lay low for a week first."

"As long as you're friends of my dad, you can stay here," the Kid offered.

"We also need a third man for the job in Hayward. Me and Johnny can't handle the place by ourselves, but there's fifty thousand dollars we can lay our hands on."

"I don't want to rob no banks," the Fillmore Kid said. The Kid was barely eighteen, and had just bought a motorcycle with the money he'd made selling dope.

"Well, Kid," Snake explained, "you ain't really got a choice. Your old man is still locked up in Atlanta ain't he?"

"Until 1974," the Kid admitted.

"Well," Snake said, "I got lots of friends down there. Maybe your old man'd get hurt, you know?"

"I guess I'm gonna rob some banks," the Kid said.

And they did. They robbed two-thirds of one bank, to be exact. Johnny was the driver. Snake gave the Fillmore Kid a sawed-off carbine and the Kid covered the counter and the lobby while Snake got the cash. They got in fine and they got the money fine, but getting out and away was a little more trouble. When Snake and the Fillmore Kid got to the door, they heard Johnny start shooting. He was down in back of the Pontiac's fender, firing into three cars full of cops. Snake told the Kid to grab a teller. The Kid grabbed a nineteen-year-old girl in the Savings line. Snake put a gun to her head and stepped out into the street. The cops stopped shooting. Snake gave the girl to the Kid and put Johnny in the car. Johnny was all shot up. Snake got behind the wheel, and the Kid and the girl got in the back seat. Then they took off, with Johnny lying up against the dash.

The cops gave chase, and the escape ended when Snake turned down a dead-end street. Snake looked up and there were two pear trees growing against a fence. He and the Kid came out shooting, but the Kid left the girl in the back seat. The Kid was shot in the leg and Snake got shot twice in the arm. Johnny had half his head blown away in the front seat, but it took him six days to die.

"The cops scrambled his brains all over the window like a fuckin egg," the Kid told me later.

Before the trial, Snake told the Fillmore Kid to cut him loose. "Look, Kid," he said, "I'm a goner. I've got ten bank jobs, a car theft, a shooting, and an armed kidnaping to stand trial for. I ain't ever gonna see the streets, however it's played. You tell the cops whatever you need to get off light."

So the Kid turned evidence and got off with five years. Snake bought twenty with his first charge, and still had thirteen more judges to stand in front of. Then Snake started saying the Kid was a snitch.

That could get the Kid a lead pipe in his head before those five years were up. It was a low trick, and made us wonder what the Snake would do now.

Come morning, he was back on the line. "We're in," Snake said. And they were.

All of us were, and A Block started its food strike with that night's dinner. At lunch, everybody ate a lot of bread to prepare.

Even when we were beaten, Snake was one of the last to give up, and he didn't want to when he did. Snake was his own brand of weird, but he had enough heart to keep his feet warm.

20

We stayed on strike six days. On the fourth day, our action made the papers.

On the fifth day, the Sheriff met with the press. "Gentlemen," he said, "I invited you here today in order to reassure the public. The Sheriff's department has the situation well in hand. Thus far, there has been no violence but the situation is touch and go."

We laughed when we read the story in the paper. "What's that son of a bitch think we gonna do," Big Al chuckled, "stab the mush when they try to stick it through the door?"

We laughed, but we were hungry. We were hungry when we were eating, but now that we weren't, we all got the slobbers when they brought the food down the hall. The cops escorted each meal.

"Anyone who wishes to eat will be given protection," they announced over the mush wagon. We let the mush sit right where they left it. We let the soup and the noodle paste sit too. On the morning of the sixth day, the cop brought fried eggs and bacon.

"Hot eggs," he said.

We watched the over easies shrivel on the plates the cop left inside the door. It was like a death in the family, but the strike lived. We only lost two men in Number 4. The rest of us were just hurt and fading. When the trusty came by to pick up the plates and garbage, we lost a lot more.

"Did you hear what that trusty said?" Penny Candy shouted.

"What's that?" I answered.

"He says they're gonna give us steaks for lunch. Man, I ain't had a steak in a year and a half." There was saliva dripping off Penny's words.

They brought the steaks just like the trusty said, but first they brought the Sheriff himself. None of us had ever seen him before. He looked like a 250-pound light-bulb turned on its head and dressed in a suit. His shoulders were half as wide as his ass, and his head twice the size of his feet. And the Sheriff seemed to be drunk. From what we'd heard, the Sheriff was drunk most of the time.

"Men," he said, leaning at a slight tilt in the middle of the hall, "we have decided to return your visits."

After the announcement, the Sheriff left with the quickest walk his tiny feet could muster. He walked like a dancer in snowshoes. When his wobble got to his shoulders it shook his tiny head like the clanger in a bell.

We ate the steaks. The cops brought a reporter in to watch us. He took notes and everybody ate except Big Al. He said he wasn't hungry, but started eating again the next day when the cops returned to serving mush.

That's all that happened the next day. It was a visiting day, but none of us got to visit.

"A double-cross," Big Al said.

Rufus asked the sergeant. "Hey," he said, "we're supposed to get visits today. The Sheriff said so."

"That don't start until next week," the sergeant answered.

"But the Sheriff said . . ."

"The Sheriff said you could have em back, he didn't say when." The sergeant was smiling. His grin was as wide as the Sheriff's ass.

"A double-cross," Big Al stormed. Then he threw a tin cup at the wall. It clanked, and fell dead.

21

We tried to get it back but we couldn't. We called for the strike again but it didn't come. We whistled and shouted but there was next to nothing. It was mostly just Number 3 and Snake down in Number 1. Everyone else ate. They ate quietly, but they ate. We stuck it out for another day and a half, and then I was gone.

That's the way it is in the custody of the Attorney General. One day you're one place and the next day you're someplace else, and nobody asks you if you want to move, nobody even gives you any warning. They just come and you go.

The trusty showed up at noon with my street clothes. "Get your shit ready to travel," he said, and tossed in my Levi's.

Right then I began learning another one of those important lessons. People who don't live where they belong can't really afford to miss anything they leave behind. While I changed out of my oversized denims, I wanted to stay with Big Al and the rest. I knew them. I liked them.

I wanted that for about thirty seconds before I realized I couldn't afford to. In prison, you have to think like you're in a room by yourself while you live in piles. Everybody does his own number. Otherwise, you'd spend all your time missing folks, and that would eat you alive.

22

The marshals took Rufus, McGee, and me together. We each got a chain through our belt loops. Then we got handcuffed to the chain and leg-ironed to each other. Then we got in the back seat of a Chevrolet, then on Interstate 5 to 99, and south into the desert. I saw the first sun I'd seen in a month. The Zoo had left me looking like refried death.

It was August and we rode to Bakersfield and then cut east. Rufus was ironed to McGee, and McGee was ironed to me, and we weren't going anywhere except where the marshals wanted.

The law sat up in the front seat wearing ties and shoulder holsters. They took turns driving until they decided to put up for the night out in the middle of the Mojave. We were stashed in the local jail. That's where we met Billy Rose. After we were settled, each in a five-by-seven, the cops brought him in from the tank up by the sergeant's desk. He'd gotten in a fight with the turnkey about how much milk he was supposed to get with dinner, so they stuck him back in a cell.

There's not a whole lot to tell about Billy. He was a kid, maybe nineteen years old. And he didn't talk much. All I ever heard from him was that he was on his way to Oklahoma City to stand trial for stealing a car. That's all I ever heard.

The next morning, before the marshals came to move us on, the hacks found Billy Rose in the cell where he'd been left. He was by himself, but the cell had a double bunk. Billy took his sheet and tied it to the top bunk. Then he put the sheet around his neck and leaned forward on the bottom bunk until he strangled himself. It must have taken a good fifteen minutes to die that way, but he didn't make a sound. First thing I heard about it was from the cops in the morning.

"Jesus Christ," they said, "look what this son of a bitch did."

Billy was dangling in his cell like a chicken in a butcher's window. When they carried him out, his head hung over on one side, bobbing with the steps of the police. His skin had turned the color of egg whites. Billy Rose left a note the trusty found on his bunk. It read like this: "Don't give me no more shit, just send me home where I belong."

Rufus, McGee, and I continued on our way east an hour after the cops found Billy. We didn't say much, and we never went back to any of the places we left behind.

Part Two
MINIMUM SECURITY

August 1969-March 1970

```
Harris, David Victor
height: 6'2''
weight: 170 lbs.
hair: blond
eyes: blue
scars, marks: 2'' left knee
birthdate: 2-28-46
sentence: Federal, 3 years,
          refusal subm.
          induct.
assignment: Barracks 4
            Mountain 2
custody: minimum
eligible parole: August 15, 1969
parole granted:
good time date: August 22, 1971
release minus 180 days:
      Jan. 16, 1972
maximum release: July 15, 1972
```

1

Arizona is where the marshals dropped me. God and the government know what they did with Rufus and McGee. I never saw them again.

The Chevrolet took most of the day climbing a range of mountains and then dropped into a sandy valley that spread east like a griddle. After two hours of mesquite and mashed jackrabbits on either side of the dotted line, the marshals turned onto a county road running toward the next chain of hills. Fifteen miles farther, we pulled into the gravel lot marked SIBERIA, ARIZONA: FEDERAL PRISON CAMP. It had been a hundred and ten degrees all day.

"They ain't gonna lock you up," Rufus grunted, "they gonna fry you."

Rufus and McGee tried to laugh, but the best they could muster was a spit out the window; it sat on the hot rocks and cooked until it was thick as jam.

I wasn't doing a whole lot of laughing myself. I wasn't talking a lot of shit, either. Mostly I stared out the window until the marshal opened the door and undid me from McGee. Then I stood up. My hands were still chained to my waist and I wobbled until I got my balance. I was thinking real hard.

Until then, I hadn't snapped to the dimensions of my future. Trying to stand in Siberia's gravel lot, understanding came in a rush. It was something I already knew but hadn't quite dealt with face to face.

"They plan to hold onto your ass for a while," I said to myself.

I looked at the cluster of buildings and the low stone wall.

"They've got to be kidding," myself said back.

2

They weren't.

In Siberia, my time hit its stride. It was like the judge's sentence was an ocean I'd set out to cross. As I moved into the mass of my time, I could still see the shore I'd left. I was standing there, waving good-by to myself. After a while, I was a bump on the horizon, and then the I left behind me was nothing much at all, just someone I'd once been, stranded on the edge of a long stretch of days and weeks with signs of the Attorney General everywhere.

Sometimes I swore I wouldn't let it make me different, but it did. Before, I'd always done the things I cared about and cared about the things I did. Those options were no longer available. I was on someone else's time, twenty-four hours a day. Living that way, I was to discover, has consequences. Right away, life gets a lot stiffer.

The Attorney General likes to shape his days into nice tight bunches. I'd always been a little looser myself, but I didn't have much choice. It's called the Program and Siberia had its own special version.

3

The Program is supposed to cure your ills and make a better man out of a bad one. "Rehabilitation" is the word the caseworkers like to use. What that amounted to was mostly work.

Five more miles up the rise in back of Siberia, mountains jerked out of the badlands valley, and ran all the way up to 10,000 feet. In those mountains was a national forest, and in the forest, convicts were helping the Arizona Department of Highways build a road. The prison supplied labor and the state supplied tractor drivers, mechanics, and a road boss who usually passed out in his pickup truck before noon and slept the rest of the day. The road hadn't made a lot of progress in its history. It was begun as a fifteen-year contract to build ten miles of a two-lane highway. By the time I drove up with the marshals, it had become a thirty-five year contract with a little better than two finished miles to show for all the effort. The last half mile of cut was fifty feet off the surveyor's line.

At 7:30 every weekday morning, the Program began.

Crews of convicts lined up with their keepers and reported for work on the road. After being counted, we
were loaded in the back of trucks and driven into the
mountains to swing picks and shovels, and chop down
trees. We were back in camp by 4 in the afternoon. At
4 in the afternoon, every convict in this federal prison
system was counted, sitting on his bunk.

We were also counted three times at work and again
on our bunks at 7:30 and 9 P.M. After 9, we were confined to our barracks. At 10, the cop came by, counted
again, and turned the lights out. From then on, it was
once an hour with a flashlight until the bulbs lit at
6 A.M. If the cop ever came up short on his count,
sirens went off, bells rang, and search parties were
organized. Teams of trackers used jeeps to comb the
desert and look for telltale escape signs.

The most telltale of them all was the footprint. We
all had convict shoes, with a notch cut in the heel to
make us trackable. I was issued my guaranteed trackable footwear at 5:30 P.M., as soon as my papers had
been shuffled in Siberia's front office.

The cop walked me out the back of the administration building and down the length of the yard between
two facing rows of barracks. Each barracks held a
maximum of fifty-two men, fifty-two bunks, and fifty-
two lockers, all in a single room. Prisoners in khaki were
leaning against porches and watched us move along
the concrete walkway. We stopped at the clothing
room. That's where I got my boots, my khakis, and a
box to mail home my old clothes. After my number
had been stamped on all my issue, I was led to the
barbershop. The barber was a chocolate mail robber
named Jewell.

Jewell cut my hair down to a white sidewall under

directions of the watching cop. When the guard stepped out of the shop, the barber talked along to the clip of his scissors.

"This place ain't nothin," Jewell said, "but watch out for the Lieutenant. He be a genuine snake, even if he dumb as shit."

I listened and felt the fan blowing on the back of my ears.

4

I got to know the Lieutenant very well.

Short of the Director, he was head cop at Siberia. And he wasn't a bad guy. I wouldn't call him a good guy, either. As a matter of fact, I was never even sure whether he was a guy or not. The only thing I was sure of was that he was a cop. I was very conscious of it all the time. He was too.

The Lieutenant was also very conscious that he was five foot three. He wore a high, peaked cap and elevator shoes that jacked him up to five foot six. The Lieutenant carried a clipboard with him everywhere. And he took names. All the time he took names. If your name got taken enough times, you went to a Disciplinary Hearing.

I attended my first Disciplinary Hearing a month after I arrived. I was brought down the mountain with the lunch wagon and told to appear at 1:30 in the Lieutenant's office. The cop on the night shift had busted one of my letters to Joanie. In it I said, "The food here is shit." You aren't allowed to complain through the mails, so I had to go to the Lieutenant's office.

After the road crews left in the morning and before I returned to be heard in the afternoon, the cops searched everybody's locker. Dick Tracy sifted through mine. Dick Tracy was five foot five and had a nose that curled up on his face like a dead snake. Dick Tracy found my baby pacifier.

I got the baby pacifier the third day I was in Siberia. Chinchero, the little dope fiend who cleaned the visiting room, gave it to me. He found it under a chair. He knew my wife was pregnant. "It'll be good luck for you to keep," he said.

I threw the pacifier in my locker, where it was eventually buried under a pile of socks. When Dick Tracy unearthed it, he ran up to the Control Room. The Lieutenant and his clipboard were there.

"Sir," Dick Tracy said, "I found this in Harris's locker."

The Lieutenant stared at the baby pacifier and hefted it in his hands. "It's a baby pacifier," he said.

"I think you're right," Dick Tracy echoed.

The Lieutenant rubbed his jaw. "I wonder what he does with it?"

He tried to find out that afternoon in his office at my first Disciplinary Hearing. The Lieutenant was sitting behind the desk. Lupez, the caseworker, was sitting behind him against the wall. Dr. Jekyll was in a chair by the door.

Dr. Jekyll was the nurse. He worked for the Public

Health Service and ran the hospital. Dr. Jekyll had all the training required to check between toes at a public swimming pool. He and I didn't get along. The first time I ever saw him, he was an ascending mound of suet at the head of sick-call line. Jekyll weighed 280 pounds and his legs had been shot up in the war. He told me I was faking. He told the dudes in front of and behind me the same thing.

Sitting on one of the Lieutenant's chairs in his white pants, Dr. Jekyll looked like a mattress stuffed in a toilet bowl. He watched me as I walked into the office.

"Sit down," the Lieutenant said.

I sat down.

The Lieutenant had two pillows under his ass. He looked five foot eight sitting behind his desk.

The Lieutenant held up my letter. "Did you write this letter?" he asked.

I examined it and handed it across the desk. "It looks like mine," I said, "but I don't remember sending it to you."

The Lieutenant snapped back like a swamp turtle. "You know all mail must be read before it leaves the institution."

"Oh," I said.

Then there was silence. Or something that was supposed to be close to it. The Lieutenant was getting angry. When he got that way, he huffed through his mouth like a steam engine. The Lieutenant huffed all over the silence.

"Harris," the Lieutenant finally continued, "in this letter there is a statement, and I quote, 'The food here is shit.' Did you write that?"

"It does sound like my letter."

"You said, 'The food here is shit'?"

"It is," I said.

"It is not," he said.

"I don't see you eating a whole lot of it," I said.

"But I've watched plenty of men here eat it, Harris, and they all like it."

"How do you know?" I asked. "Have you asked any of them?"

"I don't have to," he said. "I know they like it. I watch them liking it."

"Well," I said, "you asked me and I told you it's shit. Because it is. And I wrote it in my goddamn letter."

"You wrote that letter?"

"Yes," I said, "I did."

Dr. Jekyll jumped to his feet. The room swayed toward him and he screamed. "That is in direct violation of subsection C that states, 'No letter shall be allowed to leave the institution if it contains derogatory language about said institution.'" Dr. Jekyll sat down. He was huffing great lungfuls of air in and out just like the Lieutenant. We all listened to the huffing for another minute.

Then the Lieutenant threw the baby pacifier on the table.

"What's that?" he said.

"It's a baby pacifier," I said.

"It was in your locker."

"Yes," I said, "do you need it?"

The office was sounding like a roundhouse.

"What do you use this for, smart guy?"

"It's good luck," I said, "my wife's pregnant."

"Come on," the Lieutenant said.

I tried again. "I don't use it, I keep it in my locker."

The Lieutenant smiled like a water moccasin. "We want to know what you use it for," he purred. "We'll keep whatever you tell us in confidence."

I decided to lie. "I suck on it at night when I whip my pud," I said.

The lie seemed to make them feel good. The huffing lessened, and they all smiled and nodded their heads. Except for Dr. Jekyll. He was on his feet again.

"It wasn't issued to you," he screamed. "You didn't bring it in with you. It's contraband." Dr. Jekyll sat down.

I confessed. "Yes," I said, "it's a contraband baby pacifier."

The Lieutenant leaned back. He was huffing, and smiled as he picked up the baby pacifier with his left hand. With his right, he slid his desk drawer open and pulled out a knife. It was a commando knife, ten inches long with blood gutters running along the face of its wedge-shaped blade. The Lieutenant waved it about for a while after he closed the drawer. Then he put the blade inside the pacifier's rubber ring and yanked. Then he yanked again. And again. All together he yanked six times. The Lieutenant couldn't dent the baby pacifier. His mouth was flat as a board and trembling in the corners.

"They are made out of very hard rubber, sir," Dr. Jekyll said. He didn't get to his feet to say it.

The Lieutenant listened, and went back to his knife. After three more yanks, the rubber gave, and his giant Jap sticker cut the pacifier in half. When he had finished, the Lieutenant watched my eyes while he threw both halves into the wastebasket. Then he smiled. Dr. Jekyll and Lupez smiled with him, so I smiled too. We all smiled and listened to the huffing subside.

Finally the corners of the Lieutenant's mouth stopped twitching, and he spoke. "You can leave, Harris," he said. "We will notify you of our decision."

I walked past the Control Room and out into the

yard. It was a hundred and eight in the open spots. Jewell was leaning in the shade against Number 4. I walked over to him.

"What's happenin?" he asked.

"I'm not all that sure what it is," I said, "but it sure does happen."

Jewell and I laughed. The Lieutenant and his clip-board watched us from out the Control Room window.

The next day, I was told I'd lost nine days' Good Time.

5

For me, Siberia was a game played for an elementary stake. The contest was all about what kind of person I would be. It was no easy fight. Siberia had a definite model in mind and Good Time on its side.

The Attorney General owns thousands of locks and keys and a ton of barbed-wire fence, but none of them ever came close to keeping my toes on the line the way Good Time did. Good Time made me guard myself. It made me want to be one person so I could hurry up and get out to be another. The workings were simple. If I was his kind of prisoner, the Attorney General would let me loose early. The offer was tempting, but I finally decided Good Time and I didn't belong on the same side. Good Time is fatal in large doses. After too much of it, you forget who you are. You forget the

Attorney General is an asshole, and want him to like you and treat you like a friend.

Lupez explained the system to me as soon as I got to Siberia. If things went right, the caseworker began, I'd be out of Siberia in twenty-five months, eleven days.

Over the months we spent dealing with each other, Lupez said that to me a lot. Every time he said it, it sounded like good news. However I looked at his figures, the date he came up with arrived ten months, nineteen days sooner than the one the judge stuck to me in the beginning. The difference made me want Lupez's calendar to come through, and as soon as I did, Good Time jumped me from the corner and it was a struggle for the rest of my time. I wrestled with that motherfucker as long as I was locked up. And I was always at the disadvantage. I wanted out and the Attorney General is definitely the kind of guy to use that feeling for his own ends.

I hadn't been in Siberia fifteen minutes when I was issued a string of dates computed by the convict clerk on Lupez's adding machine. The collection was known as a Time Card. Twenty-five months, eleven days was only one feature, arrived at according to the Attorney General's formula of nine days off the end of my sentence for every month I spent going along with the Program. At Siberia, we were all classified Minimum Security, and minimum securities earned a dividend close to 30 percent. The caseworker smiled and handed me my Time Card. His smile looked like an ax hiding in a slab of whole-wheat dough. As I reached for the computations, I felt Good Time grabbing at the scruff of my neck, getting ready to mount.

The Time Card had my name at the top. After the part about FBI #230 828 G, the first line read Expiration Date, with July 15, 1972, typed in. Next came

Expiration Minus 180 days, January 16, 1972. This was there, Lupez noted, because all first offenders are automatically given a shot at the streets when they get six months from the end. I allowed as how that was a nice kind of thing to have, and looked back at the card.

One line down, I read something called Expiration with Good Time and recognized the date Lupez had spoken of, August 22, 1971. I started to smile and felt Good Time jump with a rush onto my shoulders and pull the cinch strap tight. The last line was even better: Eligible Parole, August 15, 1969. I looked at the date twice to make sure. I choked a little and tried to tuck my mouth in, but Lupez knew he had me anyway. The caseworker never stopped grinning. I felt the bit slip between my teeth and understood why so many folks walked the straight and narrow. I wanted to know more about this Eligible Parole stuff.

Lupez was glad to oblige. Parole, I was soon to learn, was Good Time's big brother and the real ass-kicker in the family. It was in this area, Lupez explained, that I was especially lucky. Most prisoners weren't allowed to see the Parole Board until they'd finished a third of their sentence, but I'd been sentenced with what was called an A number. The A meant I could see the Parole Board as soon as I got situated. They might even set a release date, Lupez hinted, who knows?

I sure didn't. But I did learn quick. I was never quite the same after my first look at parole up close. Two days after the Lieutenant seized my nine days' Good Time and hacked my baby pacifier to death, I had my first parole hearing. It took fifteen minutes. The man who heard my case had a nose like a rubber ball and ears like a bat. When the hearing was over, he said they'd let me know.

And I thought about it until they did. Good Time walked me through my paces late at night on my bunk. I dreamed about doors opening, and twitched inside. Thinking I might be able to go home made me want to do it all the more. But I was doing all this wanting in a place where I couldn't pursue my desires, where I was stuck with whatever they gave me. The more I wanted out the door, the more I belonged to the man with the keys. My wants made me forget who I was and fret about what I wasn't. Folks like that are very easy to control. I stopped talking for a month and stayed out of trouble. I mostly sat on my bunk in suspense. I wondered if my dog would remember me. I wondered if they'd cut me loose in time to see the baby born. I wanted them to let me leave. After a month, I'd started feeling like someone else.

The Parole Board stopped my disintegration in its tracks. After a month of waiting to hear, I finally heard. The board said I'd best wait until next year and see them again. Lupez said he was sorry it hadn't worked out, and gave me a new computation. This one had Eligible Parole pushed back to October 15, 1970. Right away, I felt lonely and trapped. My bowels got loose and my lungs ached. In our first big fight, I'd been a fool and let Good Time carve me up with my own expectations.

When I recovered, I decided I'd have to deal with Good Time in a whole different way. Sometimes after that, Good Time worked me into a headlock but it never rode me anymore. Four months after I'd first been locked up, I threw my Time Card away. I promised myself not to let them know I wanted to leave. I figured to just hang around being whoever I had in mind, until they opened the door.

6

Aside from Good Time, the Attorney General didn't waste his best troops on us. Siberia was watched by the Prison Service's fourth string.

Tweety Bird was a prime example. Tweety was short and blond with real pink cheeks and a pair of Coke bottle bottoms over his eyes. He said they helped him see. Tweety loved to give orders. He tried to keep his voice down to a soprano, but every time he set out to bark, he chirped instead. His voice never changed and he never stopped playing hard guy. Tweety wanted to be a lieutenant very badly. He couldn't walk in a door without talking all kinds of shit and making a flock of noises like the Giant Katydid That Ate Bismarck, North Dakota.

Tweety began his career at Leavenworth but got transferred early. At Leavenworth he tried his act on two big blacks doing double lifes, and they put him in a headlock, pulled his pants to his knees, and fucked him until his asshole dribbled juice. When Tweety got the stitches out of his bowels, he was sent to Siberia to get "some experience in minimum security supervision." Tweety didn't talk about Leavenworth, but two guys in Number 3 had been there when it happened. One even claimed he got a lick in after the brothers were done.

Then there was the Fat Cop. Fat Cop started working for the Attorney General out in a California kids' joint. He had no small impression of himself and thought he'd let those little greasers know who was boss right away. Three weeks later, four youngsters stuffed him headfirst in a trash barrel. They stuffed him so hard and he was so fat that the captain had to bring the bolt cutters to chop him out. Fat Cop got sent to Siberia on the next bus.

Fred the Fed was a fuck-up too, but in a whole different way. He was my favorite. Fred started as a bright boy who liked to mess around. He got out of the navy when World War II was over, and he couldn't find a job. The Prison Service was hiring and his navy time counted toward the pension. So Fred the Sailor became Fred the Fed, and Fred the Fed figured out very quickly that he didn't take being a cop all that seriously. Fred's only problem was he wanted the pension, and Fred the Fed was lazy. So he just put in his time, and discovered he liked convicts. As a matter of fact, Fred the Fed could easily have been one himself. Fred the Fed was a hustler and a thief.

I worked on Fred's road crew, and mostly we just stole for the boss. We'd trade equipment for whisky. All told, we hid a jeep, six drills, forty-seven shovels, and a blowtorch in the woods for Fred. The Lieutenant suspected, but didn't want to prove anything because of all the sides of beef missing down at the kitchen. The Lieutenant didn't want any government inspectors around, so Fred just got put on permanent night shift.

Soon after his reassignment, Valdez ran off when Fred the Fed was on duty, so Fred the Fed was sent with the posse to catch him. Each tracker got a gun and a holster, a sack lunch, a jeep, a radio, and a canteen before heading out into the night to look for footprints. Fred the Fed went off in a direction he was sure Valdez hadn't gone. Fred just figured to spend the night out on the desert and draw hazardous-duty pay, but he accidentally found Valdez asleep behind some mesquite. In the dark, Fred almost ran over the escaped convict. Fred didn't know quite what to do, but ended up giving Valdez his sack lunch and canteen. Fred the Fed had a lot of explaining to do when the posse finally caught up with Valdez in the morning. He was sleeping in a railroad maintenance shed, and still had Fred's canteen.

Somehow, Fred the Fed managed to talk slick enough to make it past Valdez to his pension. When he reached twenty years, the Lieutenant presented him with a gold tie clip. The local paper wanted to run a story on his achievement, but Fred told the reporter he didn't want any of his friends to know where he worked. Fred the Fed later traded the tie clip to the Cisco Kid for a box wrench and a spool of wire.

If Fred was the best of the lot, Dick Tracy was without doubt the worst.

Tracy started out as the deputy in a two-cop Arizona town. Dick Tracy was short and had the face of a starving weasel. To make up for his appearance, he bought a .45 revolver in a special tie-down, quick-draw western holster, and wore it to work. It had a silver horseshoe for a buckle. Dick Tracy would walk up and down Main Street with this small cannon pulling him into the gutter and up against the parking meters. He was watching. Tracy had eyes like so many small bugs that just crawled up the sides of people's necks. Every now and then he'd stop someone on the street, jack them up against a wall, and proceed to frisk. Sometimes he pulled people out of cars and checked their papers. When folks got stubborn, Dick Tracy'd just slap leather and stick his cannon in their ear. "I just got a few questions I'd like you to answer," he'd say. He told the sheriff he was looking for the Mafia connection in town. Dick Tracy was fired after his second week.

So he went to Texas and took the tests to become a prison guard. He passed the third time he tried and was an immediate success. The first month on the job, Tracy busted one of the Mission's convicts with three bennies in his pocket. Dick Tracy got an immediate promotion and the convict got another five years. It looked like Tracy was going to be a star until the El Paso police busted him parking downtown at three in the morning with a thirteen-year-old girl wrapped around his ears. The police held him overnight on statutory rape until they found out where he worked. Charges were dropped, and Dick Tracy was sent to the towers.

The towers were exile for Tracy. He just sat for eight hours and watched a stretch of wall. Dick Tracy did well enough until the captain drove by his tower and found the guard asleep. Dick Tracy was on Civil Service and couldn't be fired, so the Attorney General just sent him out to Siberia, where it was presumed he couldn't do too much damage.

Dick Tracy liked it in Siberia. Arizona was his old stamping ground. "I used to be a sheriff in these parts," he liked to say, "until the Prison Service hired me away. I hated to leave, but go where the money is, that's what I always preached. Just a gun for hire," he'd say, and chuckle.

It didn't take long for me to want bad things to happen to Tracy. He was a pimple on my life.

7

Dick Tracy had a favorite trick he caught me with once. He carried a fuck book rolled up in his back pocket. Tracy used to drive to Nogales and buy them on his day off. The magazines were full of color glossies and cost two dollars apiece. Tracy must have owned every one that was ever printed. Each day he showed up for work with a different magazine. When he was feeling the itch, Tracy liked to hang back in the shadow like a warm slug with his book rolled up in his hand, waiting for fresh game to walk by.

Somewhere near the end of October, I walked into his trap. It was after dinner. The days were still warm and the last sun was splattering the chow hall with light. I was heading out to the yard to stand in the glare and fart. It was a common ritual and traffic was especially heavy that night. Dinner had been some kind of creamed meat, and creamed meat always left us with a lot to fart over.

Dick Tracy sprang toward me when I let the chow hall door slam. He held up his latest edition of *Body Shop* so I could see. Tracy had the book opened to a close-up of a cunt.

"Been a while since you had your face up in one of them, hasn't it, Harris?" Tracy's grin was covered with grease and razor nicks.

The vulva seemed to be covered with tufts of wire and backed by the distant face of a woman who looked like she'd sniffed the underwear of everybody in Fort

Dix. She was lying on her back and using her fingers to spread the vulva's lips. It looked like a cross between a pound of liver and an old alligator with a little Lake Erie leaking around the edges. Face to face with that cunt, there wasn't a thing I wanted more in the whole world.

"Nice, huh?" Dick Tracy pushed.

I swallowed and listened to the creamed meat commit one more massacre in my bowels. The guy next to me looked over my shoulder and almost choked. He hadn't seen a cunt in six years.

I liked to laugh at Dick Tracy, but I learned to hate him.

I learned to hate him late at night lying on my back with that sloppy woman nibbling at my mind. I was brought up to believe that hating is a very mean and dangerous thing to do, but I hated Tracy anyway. I learned to hate him because I had nothing but concrete to rub my dreams against.

On my bunk in the darkness, I swore I'd find that store in Nogales someday and burn it down to its basement.

8

My bunk was where I lived. It was mine by right. In every lockup, joint, detention center, dungeon and torture pit, a prisoner's bunk is his own turf. At least as far as the other convicts are concerned. It's etiquette to ask before you sit on someone else's bunk, and the penalties for ignoring custom are stiff. We weren't issued any privacy, but we tried to make up for it by granting everyone the right to lie up there as if they were a thousand miles away, and not get interrupted./

I did that a lot. I would sit on the sagging springs, tuck my knees up, close my eyes, and paint pictures on the back of my skull. With my eyes closed, I'd want things.

I wanted my wife. I wanted her to make it soft and easy, and I wanted all our rough spots to disappear. I wanted it to be good between us.

I wanted my dog. I used to hang out with him when things weren't right with my wife. We spent a lot of time together. He was all white, and loved to chase cows.

I wanted to be in the hospital when my baby was born. I wanted to pace back and forth in the waiting room and listen to the doctor tell me the news.

After covering the domestic issues, I broke out into a wide range of general fantasies.

I wanted a double burger, the kind we used to eat on Friday nights in high school before we drove out to the orchards to neck.

I wanted to own a big silver horse and ride for miles, up and down hills, over ridges and into the sunrise.

I wanted to live in a house with large windows, lots of doors, and a view of the Golden Gate Bridge.

After a while, when I'd gotten deep into it, the wanting always got close to the present. I wanted out the door, and after I wouldn't let myself want that anymore, I wanted to stick it to those gray-suited mother-fuckers who came by and counted every hour.

When I'd want that, my hands clenched and I

opened my eyes. Every time I did, the place looked the same. The enormous room was divided into four rows of racks, thirteen bunks a row. Each bed had a khaki blanket, and a locker next to it. The whole space smelled from the combined residue of all our armpits, half a carton of burning cigarettes, and the kitchen's latest version of creamed meat. After the lights were turned out, the room settled into a long line of bumps and a succession of noises in the night. The strangest sounds of all came from Carlos.

Carlos ran the clothing room and lifted weights when he wasn't asleep. When he was, Carlos drowned. Like clockwork, every other night. Usually, he didn't begin until after midnight. Some nights I was awake, looking out the window at the floodlight, and I listened.

"The water," Carlos would scream, "the water," so loud God Himself must have heard. Then Carlos woke up covered with sweat. He got on his knees and prayed to some holy mother in some holy place and slept easy for the rest of the night.

Night officially ended in Siberia at 6 A.M. when the lights came on. Every morning I rolled over, lit a Camel, and wanted to throttle the guard who flipped the switch.

We all did, and to this day I believe we were supposed to. It's not a hate I want to apologize for. I hated as a matter of survival. I hated because it was the natural response to the way I was treated. I hated because I couldn't afford to want and I couldn't afford not to. Not hating was giving in, and giving in was a good way to end up like the Attorney General. None of us wanted that. We knew firsthand what he was all about. He made his living putting folks in a cage, and that has always seemed to me like a low way to live.

Hating wasn't nearly as dramatic as it sounds. Not when you have to live with it each day. I used to keep my hate back where I wouldn't trip over it, back where it wouldn't strangle whatever mellow spots I had left. Hating didn't consume a lot of my time. It was just there, like the heat, holding an edge on everything. It came with the number they gave me and I wore it the same way. Like everyone else, I just did what I had to, and went out each morning intent on reclaiming some of my day, knowing I wouldn't get it all. None of us would even get most of it. But we'd get some. Hope to die, we'd get some.

It could be that Mendel the Jew got back more than anybody else. He lived one row over and closer to the door. In all of Siberia, he worked the hardest at holding his own.

9

Mendel the Jew was an anarchist and the Lieutenant's archenemy.

Mendel had been sentenced to eighteen months by a Denver judge for refusing to go into the army. Rumor had it that Mendel was going to get probation, but the night before sentencing, someone blew up the judge's garage with an estimated sixteen sticks of TNT. The judge asked Mendel about it the next day.

"Last night," he said, "the garage next to my home was blown up. Did you have anything to do with it?"

Mendel smiled. "It's not a bad idea," he admitted. Then he smiled again.

Everyone in the courtroom said it was that last smile that got Mendel off as light as he got. That plus his size. Mendel was smaller than the Lieutenant. He couldn't see without his glasses and looked like a fourteen-year-old ham-radio operator. No judge in Denver could sentence a face like that to more than eighteen months, so eighteen months is what Mendel the Jew was given.

"I'll be back," he told the judge.

Mendel still looked the same when he got to Siberia. The Cisco Kid and Jake the Barber spotted him when he first came out in the yard.

"I wonder if they let him bring his model airplanes along," the Cisco Kid laughed.

Jake the Barber didn't say a thing. He was called Jake the Barber because it sounded like a gangster's name. Jake's real name was Stanley Barbucci and he made a lot of claims to gangsterhood. Jake always drove a new car on the streets and carried a .38. The gun is what got him busted this time. They're illegal for ex-convicts to carry and Jake had done time before. This stretch was only six months long.

"When I get out," Jake used to promise, "I'm gonna have a broad carry my iron for me. Keep it in her pants where I can always get to it." Then Jake laughed. Jake laughed with his lips rolled back and his tongue stuck out so he looked like a fried egg sandwich. Jake the Barber was something of a dump truck, but he worked in the kitchen and stole meat for me on occasion, so I dug him.

Jake stopped Mendel on his way back from the clothing room.

"What'd they put a kid like you in prison for?" Jake asked through his cigar.

Mendel looked up at Jake. Mendel's eyes were so far down in his glasses that Jake felt like he was being watched from Kansas City. After staring at him until his cigar went out, Mendel pulled the stogie out of Jake's mouth.

"I'm a gangster," Mendel growled. "You'd better stay clear of me. It'll be good for your health." Then Mendel stuck the cigar back in Jake the Barber's mouth, and walked off to find out where his bunk was.

Jake the Barber loved Mendel. "Look at him," Jake used to say, "I bet he's one of them criminal geniuses. One of them child progididdies, or whatever you call em."

The Lieutenant loved Mendel too. Mendel was the only one in the camp smaller than the Lieutenant, so the Lieutenant had the urge to adopt Mendel. "A kid who looks like you can't be all bad," he told Mendel.

"If you ever call me kid again," Mendel answered, "I'll have my gang come down from Denver and blow up the water tower."

From the time he arrived, Mendel decided he wasn't going to belong to anyone. First, the Lieutenant put him to work up on the mountain with the road gangs, but the Fat Cop busted Mendel and Sam the Wood-cutter for sitting in the back of a truck whipping each other off, so they sent Mendel back down to camp.

"I know a kid like you has a lot of sexual energy," the Lieutenant told Mendel, "puberty is a difficult time, but . . ."

"You called me kid again," Mendel interrupted.

"Sorry about that," the Lieutenant apologized, but Mendel walked out of the office anyway. For the next two weeks the Fat Cop was stationed to keep an eye on the water tower, but nothing happened. "I let everybody make one mistake," is the way Mendel explained it.

Mendel got reassigned to work pulling weeds in the garden outside the Director's Office. He'd pull weeds until ten and then go over to the library and read the back issues of *Boy's Life* and *Popular Mechanics* until lunch. After lunch count, it was Mendel's habit to go out by the culvert at the parking lot entrance and go to sleep. One afternoon, the Lieutenant found him and woke him up.

"You're sleeping," the Lieutenant said.

"Not anymore," Mendel said "You just woke me up."

"Sorry about that, but I had to. Look here, Mendel," the Lieutenant warned, "you've got to understand something. You're a prisoner. You're supposed to be working. That's what prisoners do."

"I don't like that arrangement," Mendel responded.

"Well, if you keep on sleeping, I'll transfer you to the Mission, where a kid like you wouldn't stand a chance."

"You called me kid again," Mendel glared.

But it was all show. Mendel had already decided a compromise was necessary. He shifted his jaw and smiled. "You were carried away with your anger," he told the Lieutenant. "I'm an understanding man, Lieutenant. And I'm a reasonable man. I'm willing to make a deal. I'm going to keep doing what I've been doing. At the same time, I understand it's your job to catch me. So we deal. Whenever you catch me, I'll go back to work for the rest of the day."

The Lieutenant agreed, and he and Mendel launched

into a running game of hide-and-seek that lasted until Mendel left. Sometimes Mendel won because he hid all over the place, moving regularly and in secret. And sometimes the Lieutenant won. He knew the whole camp and had a lot of people working for him. The Lieutenant won enough so that Mendel had to take him seriously as an opponent.

"I've come to a grudging respect for the idiot," Mendel would say. Which is all the notice Mendel commonly gave most of the world. Except for his father. His father was Mendel's hero.

"It's a family obligation," Mendel explained. "Every son is supposed to consider his father a hero. That's what America's all about."

Mendel's father didn't appear to be a hero at first glance. The elder Mendel was shorter than his son and worked on an assembly line in Denver, making sprinkler heads. Until the German invasion, Mendel's father had been in the Polish army. Then he fled to Russia and became a Russian soldier until the end of the war. Then Mendel's father fled to West Germany and emigrated to the United States. He had worked at the sprinkler factory for fourteen years. As a young man in Warsaw, Mendel's father had spoken on the street corners for the anarchists. It was he who talked Mendel out of being a gangster.

His father came for his first visit two weeks before Thanksgiving. It was then he found out his son had become a gangster. The visiting room was packed. I was there with Joanie and I could hear Mendel and his father talking.

"My son, a gangster," the elder Mendel moaned. "My son, a gangster. For this I run seventy miles in my bare feet and crawl over barbed wire?" He stared at his shoes while he talked, as if Mendel wasn't even there. "For this I listen to dogs bark on my trail? For this I make sprinklers for fourteen years? For my son, a gangster. If your mother were alive, she would be sobbing at your feet. If Sacco and Vanzetti were alive, they would spit on you." Mendel's father wiped his forehead, and Mendel promised he wouldn't be a gangster anymore.

Gangster or otherwise, as long as Mendel was in Siberia he kept to himself. Everyone liked him and he was friendly, but Mendel just didn't talk much. He communicated a line at a time. At dinner, he ate either by himself or at a table where no one spoke English. Mendel didn't like any interruptions while he was eating. It was part of his ongoing struggle with the Attorney General. Mendel was committed to taking more time to eat than the Lieutenant wanted to give. Mendel hunched over his tray, and ate one shred at a time. He chewed each shred until it was juice. His first dinner took two hours and forty-six minutes. They had to keep the chow hall open past eight to let him finish.

"A man has a right to eat," Mendel told the Lieutenant when he tried to speed up the process. After a while, the kitchen started feeding Mendel at three in the afternoon so the chief steward wouldn't have to work overtime.

Mendel needed the nourishment. He took up weightlifting as a hobby and eventually became Siberia's lightweight champion. Once Jewell, J.C., and I passed him on the weight yard. We were on our way back from smoking a joint out on the edge of the baseball diamond. Mendel was adding five-pound weights to the bar. He nodded at us.

"What's happenin?" Jewell asked.

"Bench presses," Mendel answered, and looked back at the bar.

"Say, Mendel," I said, "I always wanted to ask you. What're you gonna do with all them muscles when you get back to Denver?"

Mendel looked up and pushed his glasses back on his nose. "Lay on em," he said.

10

As Mendel's time grew short, his arms bulged and his struggle against the Lieutenant focused on Mendel's Good Time. Mendel didn't want it. The anarchist in him refused to accept gifts from the government. With an attitude like that, Mendel managed to lose most of the Good Time he was given. All but seven days. As Mendel's release approached, he fought to lose the last of his good behavior.

His first move was straight ahead. Mendel approached the Lieutenant. "I don't want your fucking seven days," Mendel said.

The Lieutenant didn't sympathize. "A good kid like you shouldn't have to do all his time," he answered. "It's not fair."

"Don't call me kid," Mendel snapped.

"Excuse me," the Lieutenant added, but he wouldn't budge. Mendel's Good Time was his for keeps.

But that didn't stop Mendel. Mendel decided to

grow a beard. Growing a beard was strictly forbidden. It took Mendel two months, and even then it just looked like a cat sat on his face.

"Having a beard is against the rules," Mendel informed the Lieutenant.

"What beard?" the Lieutenant said. "Kids your age can't grow beards. It doesn't happen until later in life."

"Don't call me kid."

"Excuse me," the Lieutenant added.

"No," Mendel growled. "You need a lesson. Bye-bye water tower." Mendel turned on his heel and walked back out into the afternoon.

That night, the Fat Cop went back to watch the water tower.

The Lieutenant was running scared, but it was a small victory for Mendel. Mendel the Jew had only two more weeks to go, and he was getting desperate. Mendel shaved his beard and painted another one on with shoe polish. Then he started standing on his head whenever the cop came by to count. It was a flashy move on Mendel's part, but basically worthless. The Lieutenant continued to ignore him.

Three days before his release, Mendel took a pile of rocks he'd collected, painted them white and spelled out FUCK on the visitors' parking lot. The Lieutenant had the rocks collected and ground up in the rock crusher. Mendel was close to tears. Before he could regroup, Mendel was released.

The Lieutenant was by the front door when Mendel left. His last victory over Mendel the Jew had mellowed him. He'd put on a little weight and smiled down at Mendel.

"I'm not through," Mendel said. "I've got a judge to

deal with in Denver, and then I'll be back. Someday you'll be downtown and you'll see me, and I won't be alone. I won't forget you, Lieutenant," Mendel promised. "I remember like an elephant." Then Mendel left.

The Attorney General issued him a suit, but it was too big and Mendel had to roll up the cuffs. The pants legs covered his feet so he looked like he was walking in buckets. The last thing I heard, Mendel got to Denver, burned his suit, and started working with his father down at the sprinkler factory.

11

I was a little bit like Mendel, playing the game by myself. But that was mostly when I was on my bunk or in a mood. The rest of the time, I ran in packs like everyone else.

Convicts do that because it fits their situation. Any man in the hands of the Attorney General needs friends close by. In small groups, prisoners look out for each other and share the weight. That makes all the difference in the world. Hanging out with your friends gets jail feeling as close to home as it ever can. I hung around with J.C. and Pablo, Jewell, Hot Stuff, Curly, Tom Sawyer, and Ulysses S. Grant. In a mass or smaller bunches, we spent time together, sometimes walking around the yard, sometimes talking, sometimes just standing around, not saying much and looking for ways to entertain ourselves.

There wasn't a lot of regular entertainment in Siberia. What little there was centered around Slick Willy and the Parade.

Slick Willy ran the gin game in Number 4. He was fat as six bears in winter and wore his hair up on his head in a kerchief like a mammy. After Willy got off work, he stripped to his underwear and headpiece, and held court at the table by the heater in the game room. Folks used to come from all over Siberia just to watch Willy play. Willy handled cards with style. He'd play anybody for whatever goods they'd gamble, and won a lot more than he lost. Slick Willy's meat was the Car Salesman.

Every night until lights out, and sometimes later in the bathroom where the light was still on, Willy helped the Car Salesman lose his shirt. He lost two watches, a ring, and forty-six cartons of cigarettes to Willy, but he kept coming back for more. The Car Salesman's wife, a secretary, brought him money every weekend. He lost it by Wednesday. Thursday and Friday, the Car Salesman gambled on credit.

"Don't like to take credit," Willy'd say.

"Come on, Willy," the Car Salesman would plead, "you got to give me a chance to win it back. I feel a streak comin."

Once a week, Willy'd let the Car Salesman win. That was the extent of his streak. Usually, Willy let him win on Friday night. When he did, we could always tell it out in the Parade. The Car Salesman would walk onto the front steps of Number 4, just before count at nine o'clock. In good weather, that time of night, there were always six or eight people mingling around the steps. "Beat the son of a bitch so bad he had to go to bed early," the Car Salesman would say. Willy'd sleep until noon on Saturday.

When we weren't watching Slick Willy and the Car Salesman divvy up the Car Salesman's fortune, we were in the Parade. The Parade started after all the late eaters finished farting in front of the chow hall. Mendel was always the last one done. He usually kicked the Parade off by walking up the concrete walkway to the front office and turning left. He'd follow the walk back around its rectangle past the chow hall with a left turn at the library, and the Parade began. Before we were put back in our barracks for the night, everybody made an appearance. Sometimes alone and sometimes in groups of six, nearly three hundred convicts did a few laps around the perimeter. Between laps, we hung out on the steps or in the middle of the yard where the TVs were mounted eight feet up on posts.

The Parade was never complete until the Lizard arrived. He usually got into the action late, but he got there most every night. Until it died, the Lizard usually brought his toad along for an evening walk.

12

The Lizard ran Siberia's greenhouse, raising plants for the gardens in the guards' housing project on the other side of the parking lots. He caught his desert toad on the banks of Siberia's sewage pond. The Lizard trapped flies to feed it, and kept his pet in with the plants. When he brought it out at night, the Lizard's toad wore a leash. The Lizard walked with a cane and kept good pace with the toad.

"Got to give the ugly fucker his exercise," the Lizard explained.

The Lizard was some kind of dragon in the Texas Klan. He walked the toad around the yard a couple of times, and then took it back to the greenhouse. When the Lizard returned, he walked down to the far end of the yard and hung around with the rest of the East Siberia Patriotic Association. The association included a good number of snitches, not to mention police. The Lizard was their leader.

In September, he painted his cane red, white, and blue stripes. Painting it that way was an unmatchable act for the rest of the membership, so the Lizard was automatically president. Even with a regular cane, his work for the Klan made him the natural leader. His followers included the Fat Cop whenever he had yard duty and the Car Salesman whenever he wasn't in with Slick Willy. The Car Salesman missed a lot of meetings. The rest of the membership varied. Dick Tracy caught it whenever he could, but mostly it was just Big Red the Snitch, Tiny Tim, and Officer Murphy who made it every night. Officer Murphy was a customs cop who got busted dealing the stolen furs he'd just enforced the law on at the border. The judge gave him five years and the Parole Board cut him loose after one. For those twelve months, Officer Murphy was at the far end of the yard with the Lizard at least five nights a week. He figured the Lizard an influential man and would protect him.

The Patriotic Association usually talked about the

communists and the niggers. Some nights they talked about the wetbacks, too, but they were divided on the subject. The Lizard liked wetbacks because they worked cheap and didn't talk English. But Officer Murphy was a union man and hated cheap labor, especially when it didn't talk so you could understand it. Whatever their differences, the association approached the world with a solid front. The niggers, communists, and wetbacks made up the rest of Siberia's population so, needless to say, the East Siberia Patriotic Association didn't mingle a lot. Just about the only time they got together with everyone else was to watch the football games on TV. Every Sunday, the set in the auditorium was turned on, and half of Siberia went in to watch.

In October, the Dallas Cowboys played the New York Giants, and later that same day, the Lizard's toad died. The Lizard was a Cowboy fan and shouted shit about stomping the New York niggers from the opening kickoff. He hoped to spur the Cowboys on. In the first half, they needed all the help they could muster. The Cowboy offense couldn't move, and fumbled whenever it got half a chance. The Lizard got quiet and itchy and took to making long sucking noises in his throat and spitting into his bandana. He used up two handkerchiefs in the first half alone. The Giants' Ron Johnson was picking up ten yards a shot before Bob Lilly could catch him. The first two periods ended with the Cowboys down by twenty-one points.

The second half went the other way, and the Cowboys came back. The Lizard's team scored three touchdowns and a field goal, and led with three minutes to play. The Lizard was crowing like a rooster. When the Giants were on the Cowboy 35 and moving, the cop came in, blew his whistle, and ran us out of the auditorium. It was time to be counted. The last play I saw, Johnson got three down to the 32, and it was second down. When the count was finished, the game had been over for fifteen minutes.

I had to wait for the evening news to find out the Cowboys had won. The Giants were third and four when Bob Lilly threw the Giant quarterback for a seventeen-yard loss. Then he blocked the field goal attempt, and the Cowboys ran the clock out. The Phoenix sportscaster called it one of the wildest games of the season.

We all blamed the excitement of the game for the death of the Lizard's toad. The Cowboys' narrow escape pumped the Lizard full of adrenalin and he had a hard time calming down. He hardly ate any dinner and looked nervous out on the yard. It was easy to tell when the Lizard was keyed up. When he got that way, the Lizard tortured things. He started by jamming his cane into an ant hole, but that didn't seem to help much. Next, the Lizard found a beetle by the library steps and turned it on its back. After poking the bug with a stick for a while, he hobbled to the greenhouse as fast as he could go. We never saw the toad again.

On Wednesday, the Cisco Kid approached the Lizard about it. "I don't mean to butt in," the Cisco Kid said, "but did something happen to your toad? He hasn't been around lately."

"It died," the Lizard admitted.

"How'd it happen?"

"Don't know," the Lizard claimed. "I found it in the greenhouse. Looked like its legs fell off and it musta died from the shock."

The Parade was never quite the same after the toad died.

The East Siberia Patriotic Association seemed to lose

a little of its spirit. The Lizard painted his shaving kit red, white, and blue, but they never managed a good-sized meeting again until they read about the riots in East St. Louis. Even that meeting was a smaller crowd than the ones they had when the toad was alive.

13

The Lizard never replaced his pet. The Cisco Kid tried to sell him a matching pair of toads, but the Lizard wouldn't buy. After he caught them, Cisco figured to charge the Lizard ten cartons a piece. He didn't figure on the Lizard being cheap, but he was.

"I caught the last one," the Lizard said, "and I'll catch another if I want it."

"How about five a piece, ten for the whole package?" Cisco bargained. It did no good. The Kid couldn't move the toads with anybody. Cisco kept them in his locker while waiting for the market to pick up. He figured having a toad would catch on, but it never did. We called his bunk the Used Frog Lot. Cisco held on for two weeks before he went out of business.

"All merchants have a little lost merchandise," he explained. "Besides, they shit all over my T-shirts."

For the next week, Cisco sold slightly damaged T-shirts for a pack a piece. The Cisco Kid was a walking department store. He sold roast beef, thick wool socks, and polished turquoise to use in the hobby shop. For a carton, he'd smuggle a letter without the cops getting to read it, and for two cartons he'd get you one of Dick Tracy's fuck books. This kept him smoking, but his main line of profit was tattoos. They cost twelve cartons a piece, and he was good. The Cisco Kid worked with three sewing needles taped to a broken toothbrush handle. His masterpiece was a rat's tail on Carlos's ass. It poked out between his buns and curled up on Carlos's right cheek. Rumor had it that Fred the Fed smuggled in Cisco's India tattooing ink, but I never knew for sure.

I wasn't even sure why I ended up buying one. Maybe it was the price, but I don't think so. It was bigger than that.

14

After we'd become friends, the Cisco Kid offered me a tattoo for three cartons of Camels. I think I took him up on it because of the point I'd reached. I wanted to mark myself. I wanted to inscribe my changes where I could see them in the mirror, and look the part I was playing.

It wasn't a role I was used to. I'd been raised to make progress, but Siberia wasn't one of those make-progress situations. Survival was the name of the game there.

Like all survivors, I learned during my first five months in jail to use my scars as decoration.

I had to make use of them somehow. It was too late to worry about being touched by my environment. My insides were already marked. My past life had passed from sight. Until November, I dreamed about scenes on the street. I slept my mind out on fields and along avenues. By the time the weather got crisp, my dreams were as close to the Attorney General as the rest of me. It was like being locked up had finally soaked through. While I slept, the characters of my life acted in underground garages, behind fences, in basements, and under lock and key. My body had slimmed out working on the road gang, and my skin had begun to get thick the way it does out on the desert. I'd become a functioning part of where I was. I chose an eagle to announce the fact. I had the Cisco Kid inscribe the national bird on my left arm.

The whole process took three days. Since tattooing was 100 percent against the rules, the Kid had to work in spurts, snatching an hour here and there when the cops weren't close. By then, I'd been promoted to mechanic's assistant up on the road, so Cisco and I constructed my tattoo in the parts trailer down by the welding station.

Cisco worked with a smooth motion. He used his right hand to wield the needle, and wiped with his left. Stab and wipe, stab and wipe, in swift short strokes topped by a steady line of chatter and "hold stills." The Cisco Kid wiped when the blood on my arm got too thick to see his progress. J.C. stood on the trailer steps, watching out for the law. After each session, the Kid wrapped my bicep in gauze and told me not to get it wet when I washed. Ten days after he applied the finishing touches, the scab flaked off and I had an eagle for life.

I've never regretted it. The Kid was an artist, and made me feel right at home.

15

The Kid's biggest worry in it all was my neighborhood. I bunked on the other side of Snitch Alley along the back wall of Number 4. It wasn't the best spot to live, but nobody gave me a choice. The first six bunks on either side of the row were full of loose-lipped slugs. If they got word of what Cisco and I were up to out in the parts trailer, it would mean an abrupt end to the heart of the Cisco Kid's financial empire.

Tiny Tim was the worst of the lot. He was a fat son of a bitch, his heart pumped shit and he ate his mother's pussy. He was not looked upon with a lot of love. Tiny had started snitching as soon as he was busted. He turned evidence on his first crime partners, and they got ten years a piece. Tiny got probation, but even under that he couldn't stay straight. His probation was violated for the burglary of a gas station, and Tiny was sent to the Hut in Indiana. Behind bars, Tiny was scared shitless about what he'd done for the DA's office back when the trial was going on. Word about Tiny had preceded him and there were a few folks around the yard who wanted to chop his ass up. In self-defense, Tiny ran to the arms of the police, and the dog-watch captain filled up the Hole with men Tiny said threatened him. The next day, Tiny Tim was on his way to Siberia. The Attorney General must have figured 1,500 miles was enough distance to keep Tiny safe. He was right for a while, and during that while Tiny did everything but wear a badge. He never got wise to my tattoo but, according to rumor, Tiny was the one responsible for the Cisco Kid losing his job.

The Kid worked weekends in the Corporation Yard across the road from the Hack Quarters. On the surface that sounded like a bad deal, but it had fringe benefits. The Kid got two extra days of Good Time a month for his effort. He was rebuilding engines from the big D-8 Cats we used to cut into the mountains. The Corporation Yard had an enclosed shop and a wood stove. Since there was nobody to watch him, Cisco was in the habit of holding court there on the weekends. His act came to a screeching halt two weeks before Thanksgiving. According to talk around the yard, Tiny slipped up to Tweety Bird and told him it might be a good idea to go across the road and check in on the Kid.

When Tweety opened the workshop door, he was immediately suspicious. The Cisco Kid was standing at the end of the work bench and he wasn't alone. Dr. Jekyll's daughter was propped up against an engine block with her legs wrapped around the Kid's butt and the Kid was off into it, kicking his heels and holding onto the saddle for dear life.

Dr. Jekyll's daughter was famous around the yard. You might even call her a legend in her own time. According to the story the Cisco Kid told, she'd fucked all of eastern Arizona and large parts of New Mexico and Texas. She lived a hundred yards from the institution and thought convicts were mean, torturous, mad animals with a constant bulge in their pants. This impression came largely from the back issues of *Saga* and *Police Gazette* she hid in her bedroom. Prisoners excited her and she liked to watch them whenever she could. For two months, Jekyll's daughter noticed the Cisco Kid walking by himself across the road and into the Corporation Yard workshop. Finally she decided to do a little of this *Police Gazette* stuff herself. Dr. Jekyll's daughter took an old spark plug with her.

"Do you think you could fix this for me?" she asked when Cisco opened the workshop door.

God knows the Kid tried, but Tweety got there before he could finish the job.

"Hello there, officer," the Kid said. "Just fixing the lady's spark plug." Cisco stepped away from the bench with his stuff sticking straight up in the air like a shovel, and handed the spark plug to Tweety Bird. Dr. Jekyll's daughter pulled her dress down and ran home.

The Lieutenant threatened to send the Cisco Kid to the Mission, but Dr. Jekyll's daughter said she'd tell some stories if he did, so they settled on taking away the Kid's weekend employment.

I never found out for sure that Tiny Tim was the one who clipped Cisco's wings, but I don't have a doubt about the case of my friend Curly. Curly was Tiny Tim's bust from the get-go.

16

I was out in the visiting yard when it happened.

The visiting room and the small yard attached to it were in front of the administration building behind a door down the hall from the Control Room. A hallway ran along one of the yard's boundaries and up to the Director's office. No convicts were allowed in the hall on the weekends. Except Tiny. The police let him wander around up there and loiter next to the windows looking out on the visiting yard. One of Tiny's regular positions was with his face mashed up against the glass so hard it looked like a snail crawling up the side of a fishbowl. If Tiny saw anything worth reporting, he ran to the Control Room and filled Dick Tracy in. Tiny was watching real close on what turned out to be Curly's fateful day.

Curly was in the sunny corner of the yard, visiting with a couple of dudes from L.A. and his woman. I was close by with Joanie. She was eight months pregnant and sat on the folding chair like a moored blimp.

"You're huge," I said.

"I know," she answered. There was a pinch of disgust sprinkled on the edge of her voice. "I have to wear these tents all the time."

"When's it gonna happen?"

"December," she said.

"Far out," I said.

We had that exchange twelve or thirteen times and that was just about all there was to the visit. There wasn't much else to talk over. She could tell me that her mother got a new car, and I could tell her that Slick Willy slapped the shit out of Marvin the Pimp behind the chow hall, but neither of us could make much sense out of what the other said. She'd tell me that I wasn't going to be there when the baby came, but I already knew that. Then she'd tell me she was scared, but I knew that, too. The Cisco Kid didn't sell any five-day passes, so there was nothing much I could do.

"There's nothing I can do," I said.

"I know," she said. Then she cried.

When she did, we held onto each other and felt close for a while. Over her shoulder, I could see Curly and his visitors.

They were sniffing DMT out of a little tube his woman brought with her. When the tube got empty, the four of them lay back and watched the wall where the drinking fountain was. Curly set the tube down on the bench and smiled. His grin inflated his face.

The crunch came an hour later when visiting hours were over. All of us stood in a line by the Control Room waiting to be frisked, one by one. Curly was in front of me and we could both see Tiny Tim whispering to Dick Tracy. Tracy came straight at Curly like a dog running up its leash.

He jammed Curly's head back and pried his eyelids up with his thumb. Tracy shined a flashlight in Curly's pupils.

"You're high," he said.

Curly said nothing back.

Dick Tracy returned to the Control Room for a word with Tiny Tim. Then he went out to the visiting yard and came back with a tube.

Curly turned to me. "Catch ya later," he said.

The tube was almost empty, but there was enough smell left to bust Curly. That night they shipped Curly over to the Mission, where he stayed in the Hole for eight months.

Tiny and Dick Tracy were laughing about it after dinner. Jewell and I walked past the Control Room and saw them yukking it up. All of Curly's property was in a box behind the desk, and Tracy and Tiny were reading the letters he'd saved.

"Listen to this one," Dick Tracy chuckled and read aloud: "I miss the way it would get all warm and we'd take the sheets off . . ."

Tiny laughed. Leaning on the counter, he looked like a beached whale.

"Someone ought to kill that fat sucker," Jewell said.

Someone tried to, but that wasn't until a month after Curly left, and for another reason.

17

I missed Curly. I liked him because he kept his shit right in his back pocket where it was supposed to be. You could always count on Curly to carry his weight and a bit more. I'd known Curly on the streets and he'd always been that way.

I especially missed him on the basketball court. I thought he was the best basketball player in the camp. The ones who thought he wasn't thought either the

Comanche or I was, but we both agreed he was the top of the heap. He was one of those natural all-time, all-sports athletes. In his previous life, he'd been back-up quarterback to Gary Beban at UCLA. Curly started at defensive halfback in the Rose Bowl when he was a sophomore. Two years later, he dropped his gridiron career and walked into the L.A. induction center with Resistance on his mind. The Seagull who lived in Number 5 was his crime partner. They strode up to the desk, grabbed a stack of files, ran outside with it, and burned the pile of paper with lighter fluid on the corner of Broadway and Wilshire Boulevard. The judge gave them both three years and they came to Siberia just a few days after me.

After we settled in, both Curly and I became mainstays on the Siberia basketball team. The biggest reason we played was the travel. Two nights a week the team drove into the neighboring county and played games. We weren't bad, and we won nearly as many as we lost. Our biggest problem was height. I was the tallest man on the team and I don't quite stand six foot three. Even so, our losses weren't by much. We stayed close and didn't care all that much about winning or losing. We rode bundled up in parkas for forty miles in the back of a truck, played a basketball game, took a shower, and rode back. It was nothing spectacular, but watching Slick Willy got old after a while, and the Parade hardly happened in the winter.

The week after Curly got busted, we were supposed to go up to the kid joint at Fort Grant and play a team of guards. Without Curly, we expected to have a hard time of it. We weren't in it for prizes, but at Fort Grant we liked to play for blood. We liked to win there. Especially for the kids.

Fort Grant was a cage for those eighteen and younger. The cops were in their twenties and it was a famously mean place. If a kid was caught beating off, they gave him thirty swats with an inch-thick paddle and an isolation cell for forty-five days. If one escaped, his run earned fifty slaps of the paddle and four months in the cells to heal. Mind you, these were just kids with freckles and all that. They looked to our basketball team to get some of it back for them. We were convicts too, and an act against one was supposed to be an act against all. In our schedule at Fort Grant, we managed to do all right by them. Strangely enough, the best we ever played was that night without Curly.

The locker room at the gym was being worked on, so we dressed for the game in the isolation cell block right next door. The cops let us in the showers there. We were all quiet when the guards walked us in, and the only sound in the block was from one of the cells down the hallway behind the locked gate. Whimpers bounced along the cement. Scarface Pete called down at the noise and found out it was a thirteen-year-old who'd sassed a cop. The police had hit him with the paddle fifteen times.

When we were dressed and headed for the court, Scarface Pete stopped me in the doorway and pulled at my jersey. "They're beatin little kids here," he said in a growl. "You understand that don't ya?"

"I understand," I said.

We all must have. We played over our heads. Without Curly, the cops had us outgunned. They had a Mexican who was a dead shot from twenty feet and a big sucker who stood six foot eight. We stayed with them by running. We fast-broke as much as we could and Jewell got a good streak of points from the outside. We were only four points down when we went back to the block for half time. Most of us sat on the tile and wiped our bodies. Scarface Pete stood under one of the shower heads and gave his half-time speech. Pete was our captain. An old knife wound divided his face on the diagonal. An occasional drop fell off the shower head and onto his back as he spoke.

"I've been locked up off and on since I was fifteen," Pete began. "I was at Tracy and then Chino before the feds got me on this one. I been in a lot of goddamn jails where they treated me like a dog, but never did I ever get it like them kids back down that hall is gettin it right now. I don't got to tell you just who it is that's doin it to em. I want you to think about them kids. We got to win this for them poor little sons of bitches just like us that ain't never gonna win nothin else. We got to teach them cops a lesson they ain't gonna forget for a while." Pete stopped on the edge of another sentence, but never said it. He was crying out of the corners of his eyes.

Pete's speech kept us going. We were dog tired and the cops muscled us all around the court. With four minutes left in the game, we were down by ten and beginning to lose faith. Then the Comanche took over.

The Indian was a streak player and had been off his game until one of the cops put an elbow between his eyes. The blow seemed to set his sights straight. Just as we started to fade, the Comanche came on strong. He began driving from the point of the key. I set a pick on the Mexican guarding him and he cut into the middle as quick as he could, lifting up in a fold like a jackknife. The farther he rose, the more he opened his body up into a long flight toward the bucket like a swan. Comanche ducked under the big cop's arm and bounced the ball through the hoop so tender he might have been stacking eggs. He did it four times in a row and we were back in the game. When he slacked up a bit, Pete and I began to hit from the corners. We stole the ball a lot and looked for the Comanche at the top of the key. He did the rest. We beat the cops going away, 104 to 98.

All of us cheered the Comanche in the cell-block shower. He gave all the credit to Scarface Pete, so we cheered Pete too. So did the kids on the block. One of them burned his mattress to celebrate. Jewell smuggled some cigarettes to the youngsters through a tear in the wire mesh around one of the outside windows, and we boarded the truck for Siberia.

The ride back was a cold son of a bitch. The air was thick with frost that crusted along both sides of the road. The sky was clear and full of stars, but that looked temporary.

"There's gonna be snow," the Comanche said. He was sitting on the truck bed with his back against the cab. "See the ring on the moon? That's how you tell."

18

I stared out the back. The game had lightened me up after a long stretch of being down. Ever since my last visit, I'd been having a hard time. Joanie was so swollen up when I saw her that I thought she'd drop the kid right there. I couldn't get my mind off her belly. There was a baby there, it was mine, and most of the time I couldn't think of anything else.

For a little while that night, I broke out from under my cloud and just listened to the wheels eat up the frozen road edge. At sixty miles an hour, the motion of the truck made a sound like bread breaking. That night, I fell asleep as soon as I got back to my bunk. Even Carlos didn't wake me up when he screamed. That night, I dreamed the Cisco Kid tried to sell me a pair of pearl-handled .38s. "For your kid," is the line he used.

19

The storm Comanche predicted was on us two days later. It got cold enough to freeze bare hands to a wrench, and didn't change much for the rest of the winter. It was December, and we were going to work in army parkas and two sets of wool underwear. The road was 3,000 feet in the mountains, and half the days we couldn't see fifty feet through the ground fog or the sleet. On those days, we didn't think about working. We just figured we were sent up there to suffer.

On December 2, the mechanics' lean-to half a mile from the front of the cut was locked in with sleet. J.C., the Cisco Kid, Pablo, and I huddled under the roof until the Kid took it upon himself to get us warm. He crawled under one of the D-8's and opened the valve on the diesel tank until the puddle became sizable. J.C. inched the Cat ahead and I flipped the match. The diesel fuel caught on slow, crackled, and jumped up to four-foot flames. We stood upwind from the thick clouds of smudge that drifted into the sleet, with our toes edged up to the burning puddle. We talked. Especially J.C. He told Cisco and me about the time he wrestled a bear.

"It was a righteous bear," J.C. began after wiping his nose. "Big old honey bear son of a bitch. Stood about six foot tall and weighed like a pickup truck. I really thought I was hot shit at the time. I was dealin my ass off and just scootin around Duke City in a Jaguar sedan. It was a '58 with the swole-up fenders. Used to carry a gold-plated machine pistol on the seat next to me. No shit. A shiny, fierce motherfucker. I was hot enough to fuck, and lovin it.

"I got together with the bear one Sunday when I was out low-ridin with Sweet Annie. Just cruisin. She was wearing a tablecloth and I had my top hat on, and we passed this sign set up in the corner of a used car lot. It was one of those canvas banners about twelve foot long and it said 'Watch A Bear Wrestle, $1.' I slammed on the brakes when I read the next part. The guy was offerin fifty dollars to anybody that could stay 10 minutes with the bear, so I jumped out of the Jag and took my shirt off.

"I righteously figured I could whip it," J.C. continued. "I'd had all kinds of Ranger training in the Airborne, and I can karate the shit out of most anybody. So what's a bear? Just a big, furry animal. At least that's what I figured at the time.

"This bear had a big steel muzzle and was named

Oscar. I walked out to the middle of the ring and he come out at me. When he was just about up to where I was, I grabbed his front leg, whipped it back, and gave him a hip throw. Old Oscar went over like a ton of shit. I swear, you could hear the Cadillacs bounce at the other end of the lot when the motherfucker hit. I strutted a little, and then he got up and come at me again. So I just did it a second time. He hit the mat all over again the same way, and I gave a little Ranger yell and flexed for Sweet Annie. She was standin over by the cage, laughin.

"I was too, till Oscar came on the third time. Right about then I began to notice somethin I hadn't noticed before. This bear's been watchin me. Each time I threw him, he'd scratch his head and look at me before he got up. He came a little quicker that third time. I got my hip across his body and started to bring the sucker over, and that's as far as I got. Old Oscar just picked me up in the middle of my move, lifted me over his head, and dropped me straight down. Then he pounced. Before I had a chance to squirm, he was on me like an earthquake. I was pinned so bad I could hardly move my fingers. And this bear seemed to be gettin off on it. He was snarlin and snappin and sloppin foam all over the inside of his muzzle. Oscar was growlin so loud I couldn't hear nothin else.

"Slowly I began to understand he was growlin at me. His muzzle was stuck right between my eyes, and then I remembered that bears are big, furry animals that eat people. As a matter of fact, I remember they had a reputation for eatin just about anything or anybody that got close enough to fuck with them, and that son of a bitch wasn't but a couple inches and a little window screen from me. It was then that I began screamin. I screamed like a baby and almost shit my pants. They got the bear off me, and I stuck to wrestlin with Annie after that."

The flames were down to a foot and a half now, and we moved around the puddle as the wind shifted. After J.C.'s story, we moved the Cat back and made another puddle. We lit puddles for the rest of the day.

20

When I got back to camp, I made my way through the laundry to the clothing room and tried to convince the cop there to give me a new pair of boots. Mine had started to leak. That's where Dick Tracy found me. He was delivering messages.

"Hey, Harris," he said.

I turned around.

"The caseworker says he's approved a phone call to your wife. He says to get up to his place and you can make it before count."

I walked up to Lupez's office to talk with Joanie. Lupez sat across the room and listened. Neither of us got much satisfaction. My wife wasn't home. My mother-in-law answered the phone and said my old lady'd gone to the hospital an hour before. I went back to my bunk and waited. I skipped the evening's creamed meat and spent my time inside my brain. My head spaced out and inflated to where I couldn't find the sides of my mind anymore. With my head lined up in spread formation, I took a strong look at my lives.

Every convict has his life and his other life. His life is what he gets to carry with him, and his other life is everything he gets to leave behind. In one life I was clean, warm, married, and absent. In the other, I was living, lonely, locked up, and a long way from anything I'd been. The two didn't get in touch except on special occasions. The birth of my son on December 2 was one of those. It was the first time anything like that had ever happened to me, so I paced a lot.

J.C. found me walking back and forth in the day-room. I looked up when he came in the door.

"You act like an expectant father," J.C. said.

"I am," I answered.

"I know," he said.

And that's about all the words we exchanged. I was in no mood to talk. I was captured inside a flock of twenty-acre thoughts. Finally I lay on my bunk and tried to get my head back. Fred the Fed found me there.

"You want a phone call from your old lady?" he asked.

"Sure as shit," I answered.

"Well, come on."

Fred the Fed and I trotted up to the Control Room, where Joanie was on the phone. She'd just left the delivery room.

"It's a boy," she said.

"Hot damn," I said. After being quiet for a while, I spoke up again. "How are you?"

"I screamed like a pig for a while," she said. Her voice was a whisper lined with sandpaper. "But I feel good now. I'm all wiped out. I gotta go to sleep."

I guess she did. The phone clicked and my other life disappeared back down the wire. I went back through the sleet to my bunk and sat in the dark, trying to get a picture of what had just happened to me.

To be honest with you, I couldn't. I didn't even get close. There was no way for me to figure out what being a father was. The role was a thousand miles away and I couldn't get close enough for a good look. I worried about it in the dark while the storm tried to to lift the roof off. Finally, J.C. sat up on his bunk across the way.

"You act like a father," he said.

"I am," I said.

"I know," he said and tossed a stick of weed onto my blanket. "Congratulations."

We went up to the shitter to smoke it. Everyone was asleep, and Fred the Fed wouldn't be around for another fifteen minutes.

"Kids are far out," J.C. said. "I got four of em. When they're little they shit in their pants, but other than that, they're all right. You'll dig bein a father."

"But," I interrupted, "just how am I gonna be a father in this federal motherfucker."

"Eight hours a month," J.C. answered.

J.C. wasn't wrong. I saw my son on Christmas and he did everything J.C. said he would. I dug it. That visit was just about the only all-right thing that happened from then until spring, and by spring I was in the Mission, three hundred miles farther from home.

21

Things started getting weird at Siberia's Christmas party. It was a big event. The cops rounded us all up and sent us to the auditorium. A record player ground out carols as we filed in.

When we were all seated, the music died and the Lieutenant started things off by introducing the new director. We came to call him the Rabbit. The last director had retired not long after I got to Siberia and the Attorney General had been slow with a replacement. On paper, the director was the boss boss, but I'd never met the last one. He only came back where we lived when congressmen and government inspectors came through. The Rabbit began his speech by telling us he was going to be different. He said he was a prison reformer. He didn't tell us he was a juice hawk and chickenshit to boot, but we found that out after a while. He said he had an open door to our problems and pledged us everything from better ashtrays to a real doctor. In the end, he commiserated.

"I can sympathize with you men, being here miles from your families on Christmas. I'm in the same position. My family hasn't moved out from Dallas yet and I, too, am alone this Christmas. Take heart," the Rabbit advised, "and don't get your chins down. Just work to leave here better men, ready to make your contribution."

The room echoed with the tones of creamed turkey

dinner, and the record player came back on. The cops began moving us out the doors again. Each of us was given a sack of hard candy on the way out the door. Dick Tracy was handing them out.

"Merry Christmas," he said. "Get on your bunks for count."

The holiday lasted until right after the Attorney General had finished checking to make sure no one had gone on vacation. Then the cops busted half of the Joaquin Murietta Burrito Palace.

22

The Joaquin Murietta Burrito Palace was a nice thing.

Actually, it was two nice things. First, it was a location. Just a lean-to next to a fire around the bend in the road where Tweety Bird's road crew was digging a culvert. Second, it was Jesse.

He was the part of the Burrito Palace that got busted. Jesse bought flour and beans from two dudes in the kitchen, and Fred the Fed donated chilies. Each day, Jesse put them all together into burritos. Tweety charged four burritos rent, and the rest were sold for a pack a piece down in camp. Jesse divided the profits among the Chicanos who couldn't afford to buy cigarettes in the commissary. Jesse was a philanthropist and the Burrito Palace was thought of as a community institution.

By Christmas the Burrito Palace was ready to declare its first major dividend. Jesse had been saving up, and bought a can of weed. His plan was to get every Mexican in Siberia loaded, but he never made it. Tiny Tim saw to that.

Tiny heard two Mexicans in the kitchen talking about the smoke and passed the word on. If you found Tiny Tim today, I'll bet he'd say he wished he hadn't, but at the time, he was greedy. The hacks hit Jesse's locker right after the bell rang announcing the end of count. In return for his services, Tiny Tim was the only prisoner in Siberia who got to call his family on Christmas night.

The Fat Cop and Bismarck walked Jesse across the yard. He was handcuffed to a chain around his waist, and leaning into the sleet. Jewell and I stood in the doorway to Number 4 and watched. After the car drove away, headed for the Mission with the important half of the Joaquin Murietta Burrito Palace, Tiny Tim made his call. We could see him through the administration building windows. The Attorney General had strung Christmas lights on the roof and the water tower. Tiny was leaning against the counter inside, looking warm and rosy while he talked to his old lady in St. Paul.

The Chicanos closest to Jesse got together in Number 5 and made a quick decision to pay Tiny back in kind. Rosario wanted to do it, and the rest thought that would be right since Rosario was from Jesse's home town. He planned to stick Tiny during the movie with a shank he'd made in the plumbing shop. The Christmas feature was just starting when Rosario made his move. Tiny was in the row next to the projector. I was sitting next to Pablo and J.C. back in the corner. I saw Rosario come in and sit at the end of Tiny's row. The snitch had the whole row to himself. No one would sit near him except Big Red, and Big Red was out taking a leak. Rosario moved down the line, chair by chair, until he got in range.

From where we sat, it looked like Tiny was about to be snuffed, but it never quite happened. The film broke with Rosario still three seats away, and immediately the lights came back on. While Zeno, the projectionist, mended the footage, Tiny Tim decided to skip the rest, and left Rosario all by himself with murder tucked under his shirttail. The Mexican was pissed. He figured he wouldn't get a chance that easy again.

As it turned out, he didn't need it. Sunshine took care of Tiny before he got out the door. Sunshine had spent a lot of time down at the Burrito Palace. It was his lay-around place and lay around is just about all Sunshine did. The cops tried to make him work once. They gave him a job driving the fuel truck used to fill up the Cats. Sunshine took off up the road his first day on the job, shifting to third without touching the clutch, and rammed the truck into the side of Big Red's tractor. He just lay around from then on. Sunshine was waiting by the Control Room with a piece of cake.

"Hey, Tiny," he said, "you hungry?"

"For sure," Tiny answered, reaching for the marble fudge with cocoa icing.

"Merry Christmas," Sunshine laughed.

The cake had eight hits of acid in it, and Tiny gobbled it all down on the way back to his barracks. Tiny Tim lay on his bunk, licking his fingers until he couldn't find his fingers anymore.

That lasted about an hour. When the acid took hold, Tiny jumped up and staggered out the front door, headed for the Control Room. He had his hands held out three feet on either side of his head, and he was screaming.

"My head," Tiny screamed, "my head." All the time he was looking over his shoulder. "Ahhhhhgrrrrrraaaaah," he screamed again, "ahhhhhgraaaaaa." Halfway across the yard, Tiny started slapping all over his body with his hands, stopping only to bite his fingers and hop along on one foot. He fell on his face twice before he got to the administration building. Tiny Tim collapsed through the door with a splat.

"I'm covered with spiders," he shrieked at Dick Tracy.

Tiny started to say more, but the spiders hit him special fierce so he switched to "Ahhhhgrrrrrrrrrraah" again, and twitched and kicked his legs. Dick Tracy rang six or seven bells and got four other cops to carry the thrashing Tiny to the hospital. By the time Dr. Jekyll arrived, Tiny was out someplace where no one could reach him. His only communication was a gurgle and occasional scream. Dr. Jekyll walked around the table Tiny was strapped to. He rubbed his chin and scratched his butt.

"Looks like some kind of locoweed," Jekyll growled.

"Big dose?" Tracy asked.

Tiny's eyes were bulging, and he kept shaping his mouth to blow bubbles but no bubbles came out.

"Probably shot it in an artery," Jekyll answered.

Dr. Jekyll walked to the cupboard with his white coat flapping behind him. He came back with a syringe and held it up to the light. "Seconal," Jekyll said, "it'll bring him down."

Dick Tracy agreed it would, but it didn't. The downers just turned the spiders green. Tiny's blood pressure kept rising, and he rolled his head from side to side. His eyes were closed most of the time and only opened to help him scream. "Arrrrgggghhhaaaaaaaa." The noise rattled the hospital windows.

Two hours later, J.C., Pablo, Jewell, and I were keeping watch on the hospital from the dayroom. The screams were still coming out of the sick bay in two-minute bunches. Inside, Dr. Jekyll was worried Tiny might die. The snitch's blood pressure was still on the rise. Back in the dayroom, J.C. decided to save Tiny's life.

"The dude could die of it," he said. "They fucked with his mind enough. He won't forget nothin now." Then J.C. walked out the door of Number 4 and through the storm to the hospital. He knocked on the side door. After a minute, Jekyll poked his head out.

"Is he still all fucked up?" J.C. asked.

"Get back in your unit before I put you on report," Jekyll answered.

"Give him Thorazine," J.C. said as Jekyll slammed the door.

I don't know if Jekyll did or not, but Tiny pulled through anyway. He was in the hospital for two more weeks and only came out in the yard once. His eyes were scurrying around the back of his sockets. Tiny shook his head a lot and looked all dingy and scrambled like a howitzer shell had gone off behind his eyes. On the second Monday in January, Tiny moved on someplace else. I never did find out where. J.C. and I watched him drive off with a cop after dinner.

"Merry Christmas," J.C. shouted from the corner of the library, "and a Happy New Year."

23

It was like J.C. to try to save Tiny's life. His own history had left him with a strong sense of justice.

His mother was an Indian woman with five kids. The first, J.C., was born in a converted chicken coop they called home. When J.C. was still in diapers, the family moved to Detroit and then on again and again until they ended up four blocks from Disneyland when he was thirteen. His father had long since split. His mother was keeping five kids on her salary as a waitress. She had a boy friend too. And he hated J.C. J.C. caught him whipping his mother once and told him he'd kill him if he ever did it again. The boy friend decided to move to Albuquerque, and told J.C.'s mother to come along. He also told her to leave J.C. behind, and she did. J.C. went to the mountains with neighbors for the weekend, and when he got back his mother and the other four kids had moved out.

J.C. hitchhiked to Albuquerque to find her but she'd gone on to Detroit, and J.C. was stuck in a New Mexico orphans' home. After a year, he was adopted by a fat woman and a truck driver in Albuquerque, and started getting into nothing but trouble. It all came to a head when he was seventeen. His high school teacher threw J.C. on his back in a corner and started beating him with his fists. J.C. pulled the pen from the teacher's pocket and stuck it in the teacher's chest. The judge gave J.C. a choice between the New Mexico

School for Boys and the 101st Airborne. J.C. took the Airborne and went off to boot camp.

J.C. stayed in the Airborne for two and a half years. He was a good soldier until the time of his accident. He had the accident while playing a paratrooper game. The Airborne liked to jump out of third-story windows and off roofs and stuff like that. It was considered fun and beat the hell out of lying around camp with the flies. One day J.C. took off from the third story without looking below. He landed on top of a colonel with big full birds on his shoulders. J.C. was all right, but the colonel was in the hospital for eight months. Both the officer's shoulders were dislocated, his rib cage bashed in, and one lung punctured. The colonel got a Purple Heart and a Distinguished Service Cross, and J.C. got busted to private immediately prior to his retirement as a mental case four days later.

As soon as J.C. got his discharge, he went back to Albuquerque and used his GI benefits to set up a towing service. Then he married his army sweetheart. It was fine by her, but her father couldn't dig it all. Her father was a retired Marine Corps general who ended up city manager of Dallas. J.C. was 100 percent bad news for Daddy, but she married him anyway. It was either a case of true love or extreme daddy hate; J.C. could never quite figure out which.

If it was love, it got a little hard to recognize. J.C. and his first wife didn't get along. They had two kids, but apart from that, it was all battle. She had one of those acid tongues that fork at the end like a snake's, and she rode J.C.'s ass. So he kept knocking her out.

Every time she'd get on his case, he'd tell her to stop, and then he'd tell her that if she didn't stop he'd knock her out, and then he'd knock her out. Despite the headaches, they both seemed to dig it. They stayed together for close to five years, until J.C. knocked her out twice in the same day. The first time was in front of a movie theater. They'd just gone to the show and she started riding him.

"A towing service. Big deal. A towing service," she said on the way to the parking lot.

J.C. told the kids to go to the car. Then he turned around and knocked her stone cold on the corner of Fourth and Central in downtown Albuquerque. J.C. picked up his wife, carried her to the car, and drove home. When she came to, they had a couple of drinks in the living room, and she started in again.

"Big man," she said. "Such a big man he knocks his wife out. And he's got a towing service. Big deal. A towing service."

J.C. reached across the couch and put her in the kitchen with a right cross. She ran off with a milkman from Truth or Consequences, New Mexico, on the next Tuesday.

It took J.C. a while to recover. He sold his towing service and started dealing weed. J.C. became just about the biggest hippy dealer in Duke City. He cruised with Sweet Annie in his Jaguar, shot speed, and wrestled bears. J.C. stopped shooting speed right after he stopped wrestling bears.

"I gave up on crank one day in Taos," is the way he told it. "I had a cabin up there and I was just layin around with Sweet Annie gettin a rush. Then I looked out my front window and saw six sheriffs. They had their guns out and dogs on leashes. The law made a run for the porch and the dogs started to come through the window. Then I snapped. I didn't have a window. I looked at Sweet Annie, and told her I wasn't going to shoot speed anymore. It was just too much to put up with."

But J.C. didn't stop dealing. When he got caught the first time, the judge gave him a 741. That's a split sentence; six months in, two and a half years' probation. J.C. went to the Mission for his six months, got out, and started dealing again. This time he had a partner. His partner's name was Van Pelt, and Van Pelt started messing around with a policewoman. Of course nobody knew she was a cop. She played the act well, and all Van Pelt could talk about was how she got it on. They were going to be married, and afterward she would help Van Pelt with the business. A week before the wedding, she dropped by J.C.'s to pick up an eighty-seven kilo shipment of weed. J.C. looked up just in time to see her kick in the door with a submachine gun and bring what looked like half the police in Albuquerque with her. J.C. just stood up and raised his hands. The DA gave him a choice of finishing his two and a half for the feds, or facing ten to forty in state court. J.C. took the fed beef, and ended up in Siberia with me. Van Pelt left the country.

J.C.'s sense of justice had muscle on it, but he wasn't mean. He wasn't even close. He was gentle enough to be Siberia's medicine man. When folks got sick, J.C. visited them and prescribed folk remedies he learned in Taos. His medicine worked a little better than Dr. Jekyll's, but then Dr. Jekyll's didn't work at all. It had a chance to, but Dr. Jekyll wouldn't let it.

24

Dr. Jekyll operated with a simple method. In his technique of medicine, two things are true. All your patients are convicts and convicts want medicine to get high, fake injuries to get painkillers, want to stay in bed because they're lazy, and want treatment when they are overdosed on drugs. In Dr. Jekyll's case load, this was especially true of wetbacks and communists. The technique had some incredible results. As medicine man, J.C. led the revolt against one of them in the last week of January.

It started in Number 5's shower. One of the new Mexicans was washing. He'd been brought in from the Border Patrol station at El Paso along with twenty others two nights earlier. They'd all been busted for coming across the border without permission. The standard sentencing is three months the first time, six months the second, a year the third, two years the fourth, and everything after four brings a full three. The new Mexican taking a shower was a six-month special from a village in Chihuahua. That meant he already had medical records, a fact Dr. Jekyll was soon to ignore.

The new man turned out to be an epileptic, and had a fit right there in the shower. As soon as he started twitching, his feet went off like skis and he fell flat on the floor. His lids rolled back to show his eyes riding like BB's on a ferris wheel. He was foaming when

Chinchero came and got J.C. J.C. ran across the yard
to Number 5 and pulled the new man's tongue out of
his throat. Then he sent Chinchero to get the cops. The
new guy was flopping in circles. J.C. held him but
didn't know what to do.

When Chinchero brought the cops back, they carried
the new Mexican up to the hospital. Dr. Jekyll came
over from his house and closed the door behind him.
Chinchero wanted to go inside with them, but Jekyll
told him to split in no uncertain terms. Chinchero
walked down off the steps and joined the rest of us
standing around in the yard, waiting for the news.
After a while, J.C. boosted Chinchero onto his shoulders so he could peek in the window.

"They got him tied up," Chinchero claimed.

We all scrambled for a look and we all saw the same
thing. There was one light on, and the four cops
formed a half-circle. Dr. Jekyll was the other half of
the circle. Between his wrinkled legs, we could see the
new Mexican. He was tied up with a rope. He was still
gurgling, and bouncing up and down. The Mexican
had an eye pointing at each shoulder. That was enough
to see.

J.C. ran up to the door and started pounding. After
a minute, Dr. Jekyll opened it a crack.

"What are you doin to that guy?" J.C. demanded.

"Official business," Dr. Jekyll said. "Now shut your
mouth and get off these steps."

"Official business my ass. That man's an epileptic."

"Look," Jekyll stormed, "I've been in this place six
years, and I've had to watch punks like you come up
here hopped up on goof balls and locoweed for every
day of it. Now I'm gonna find out where that dope is
comin from."

"But look at his records," J.C. argued. "He's got epileptic on his records."

"Fuck a bunch of records," Jekyll screamed. "He may be able to con some wetback doctor in El Paso, but I've seen too many of these greaseball junkies. He'll talk." Then Dr. Jekyll slammed the door.

J.C. pounded on it again, but this time the four cops answered. They all came out with Dick Tracy in the lead.

"Look, fellas," he said, "the kid's gonna be all right. It's gettin close to count, so why don't you all just hit your bunks."

Nobody moved.

"Jekyll's gonna kill that guy," Chinchero spoke up.

"Look," Tracy answered, "Dr. Jekyll's not gonna kill nobody. He's gettin treated. We just want to ask him a few questions when he's done. So move it."

Nobody moved again until Tracy walked off the steps and went over to check out the riot gear in the Control Room. Then we changed our minds.

The new guy got out of the hospital the next day. He was all right except for his left eye. It never did get quite back in line. His right one looked straight ahead and the left sort of pointed to his elbow. Other than that, the Mexican was good as new. He didn't speak English, so he couldn't answer Dick Tracy's questions. That seemed to frustrate Dr. Jekyll, but it didn't stop him. It didn't even come close.

Dr. Jekyll had just about practiced his way through February when Siberia finally lost its patience.

25

The second month of 1970 was a hard one. The road had run into granite and the Cats kept breaking. The weather came in stretches: three days of storm, two clear except for light scud up high, and then back to storm again. Some days it got so bad the road crews were kept in camp to wait out the weather, playing hearts in the dayroom. On top of that, half of us were sick with the shits and fevers. By Dr. Jekyll's standards, anything short of a hundred-and-two temperature was considered fit for work. That didn't sit well with those of us who had to do it, so we made a point of complaining as soon as we got the chance. The Rabbit was the man we had to see with our grievance.

Jewell and I stopped him as he was crossing the yard on his way to chow hall. We approached from behind his shoulder.

"Hey, Mr. New Director," Jewell shouted, "we wants to talk a second."

The Rabbit stopped in his tracks and swiveled his head to look in our direction. He waited for us to catch up to him, but never shifted his feet. The Rabbit talked to us over his shoulder for the entire conversation.

"What can I do for you men?" he asked. The Rabbit's nose twitched like a full-scale bunny, and he did a little dance step with his feet. He seemed nervous dealing with us up close.

"It's about them promises you made on Christmas," Jewell began. The Rabbit interrupted with a wave of his hand.

"I'm on my way to chow hall," he explained. "The steward tells me the new ashtrays are in, and I intend to see to it that they're on the tables tonight." The Rabbit's face broke into a grin that anticipated our breaking into cheers. As the director saw it, he'd just done us a big favor.

Jewell wasn't quite of the same mind. "That's fine and we're grateful and all that," Jewell persisted, "but what about the doctorin you was promisin. This fat sucker don't know doctorin any more than me, and he's killin us."

The Rabbit dropped his smile onto the gravel, and seemed to grind it up with his twitching feet. "Hmmmmmmmm," he said, and "uh huh, uh huh," until he finally found some words. "I'll take it up with my staff immediately," he promised. As the promise came to a close, he scurried off with a step that was almost a hop and just past a wobble.

Scarface Pete hit on him the next day with the same question. Pete had been up at the caseworker's office and decided to drop in on the director as long as he was in the neighborhood. Pete walked in without a knock. The Rabbit was behind the desk, pouring two fingers of Old Overholt into his water glass.

"It's about the doctor," Peter began.

The Rabbit flushed and didn't wait to hear the statement. "I'd love to talk more," he interrupted, "but I have a meeting with my staff. Rest assured the hospital is our first priority." With that he motioned Pete out of the room. From then on, it was a lot harder to get a hearing with the Rabbit. His open-door policy sud-

denly got crowded with schedules, meetings, and con-
ferences. The only time we saw him back where we
lived was on his way to and from the cops' dining room
with the Lieutenant for an escort. The Lieutenant
shooed us out of their path like flies.

It was finally left to Road Crew 6 to get word to the
Rabbit in no uncertain terms.

26

They delivered the message while the Rabbit was on
an inspection tour of the road.

The sleet from the day before had blown off and the
sun was up. The only snow still on the ground was in
stray clumps along the deepest parts of the roadline.
From the work site, we could see all the way across the
valley to the clouds of smoke from the Phelps-Dodge
smelter in Morenci. There were hawks flying over
Siberia. When the Rabbit's pickup approached, Crew 6
was scaling a cut. To scale, a crew with steel bars work
their way down the roadside slope attached to ropes.
Whenever they find a loose boulder, they roll it off
the slope. Scaling was Crew 6's specialty. They'd scaled
just about the whole two miles of construction. After
the Rabbit's truck passed the mechanics' shack and
headed into the cut, Manuel and Little Red sneaked
down the ridge and sent the message.

It was a seven-hundred-pound message, and it got

there quick. The message was four feet across, and that size rolls best. I heard the clatter of gravel in its wake, and started running up from the broken Cat I was working on to get a better look. The Rabbit jumped for the passenger side when the message arrived at the driver's window. It carried the truck three feet straight right, and pinned it against a tree. The message was stuck behind the steering wheel and the Rabbit was wedged against the far door. He wasn't hurt, but he had a much better look at a large rock than he'd ever had before.

"Look out below," Little Red shouted ten seconds too late.

The cops had to cut the Rabbit out of his truck with a torch. When they drove him back to Siberia in a jeep, we figured he'd picked up on what Crew 6 was trying to tell him.

If he did, it didn't show up in Dr. Jekyll's practice. As far as the hospital was concerned, things only got worse.

27

On the last day of February, Dr. Jekyll decided to do something about the high cost of medicine. To the government, that is. For starters, he decided to cut back on prescriptions. Old Mr. Gort was the first one to feel the new pressure.

Mr. Gort had been locked up off and on for better

than thirty years, and his medical records weighed almost as much as he did. Gort was in Siberia to finish up the last two years of the nickel the judge in El Paso handed out for stealing Buicks. He'd started doing time in Lewisburg in '36 and blamed his emphysema on the time he spent in the Hole there. He started having trouble with his eyes in Alcatraz, and got the first signs of arthritis in Atlanta. Old Mr. Gort had been a diabetic since he was thirteen, and picked up high blood pressure during the four years he spent on the streets in the late '50s. He slept on the bunk across from Pablo, and catty-corner from me. At night, Gort made sounds like a broken pump until he rolled over on his side. Then he made noises like a '56 Chevy dropping its transmission.

Unlike the rest of us, Mr. Gort didn't really work. Mostly he just took medicine. He had come to Siberia under orders from the doctor in . Atlanta. Mr. Gort marched across the yard every morning at nine and picked up two handfuls of pills. That was just about all he did besides read the *Chicago Tribune* and recite his medical history out loud. Gort told everyone within earshot his symptoms and what year they first started. If you were looking to drop a word in passing, the biggest mistake you could make was asking Mr. Gort how he was feeling. He usually finished his answer fifteen minutes later. Being a regular customer, Mr. Gort was on fair-to-middling terms with Dr. Jekyll. Until the first of March. That day, their relationship took a turn for the worse.

Mr. Gort showed up at the hospital for morning sick call, and came away with only a handful and a half. The blood pressure pills were missing.

"Where's the fuckin red ones?" he grilled the pill room clerk.

"I just gave out what it says on the card," the clerk answered. "Those red ones have been scratched off."

Old Mr. Gort gulped what he had with a cup of water, and set out to find Jekyll. He finally located the man back by the X-ray room.

"Doctor," he said.

"Yah," Jekyll answered.

"Doctor, the boy in the pill room musta made some mistake. There ain't no little red ones in my dose."

"Don't worry, old-timer," Jekyll began. He reached a hand onto Mr. Gort's shoulder. "You won't die. I've been looking through your records, and after looking at your readings and general condition I've decided you can go off of them. The pressure's not high enough to warrant medication."

"But they was prescribed by Dr. Moorehouse in Atlanta. Look here," Gort persisted, "I'm an old man. You cops already took my body from me. I was a bad motherfucker once, but you took all my strength. Them pills are keepin me alive. You watch, I'm gonna get dizzy without em. Always do."

Dr. Jekyll wasn't being moved. "Don't worry," he said, "you're a hearty old fella, not like these young glue sniffers. You'll hold up all right."

Mr. Gort asked for the red ones at both the noon and evening pill calls, but they weren't back on his list. He grabbed Dr. Jekyll before he left work and told him he felt dizzy. Dr. Jekyll told him to go lie on his bunk and it would pass.

It didn't. Mr. Gort lay there until lights out. I was next door reading, so he talked to me a lot.

"That dog motherfucker is tryin to kill me," he kept saying. "Goddamn real doctor prescribed them, not some fuckin government nurse like that Jekyll. You know that. He ain't no doctor. He ain't supposed to be prescribin. I get dizzy without them pills. You know that, David. I get dizzy and have trouble seein. Shit, I can't hardly see up to the shitters now, even with my glasses on."

After a night full of grunts and phlegm, Mr. Gort had his mind made up. At 9 A.M., he went looking for his medicine with an ax handle. He'd bought the weapon from the Cisco Kid for protection, and kept it under his mattress. Gort found Jekyll behind his desk, writing in someone's records. His first swing smashed the bottle of mercurochrome a foot in front of Jekyll's face. For a second, the whole office was full of red splatter. "Gimme my pills," Gort screamed.

Before the pieces of broken bottle hit the floor, Dr. Jekyll was running for the Control Room as fast as he could. His right leg was his worst, and he scraped it along like a man in a splint. Mr. Gort was huffing along behind him as best he was able, waving his ax handle. As hard as he tried, Gort couldn't match Jekyll's adrenalin pace. Mr. Gort stopped halfway to the Control Room, gasping for air. Dick Tracy was on him in a flash, chaining his hand and leading Gort away with a firm hold on his collar. They led him past Jekyll in the hallway. With his eyes the size of pinheads, Mr. Gort cast a look designed to burn a hole through the doctor.

"You're a dog motherfucker and don't know doctorin from snake shit," were Mr. Gort's parting words.

The Fat Cop drove Gort to the Mission, and the doctor there gave him back his pills. All the excitement gave Mr. Gort headaches, and it took him half a year to get rid of them. The cops should have read Mr. Gort's assault like a warning light, but they didn't.

Instead, they added insult to injury.

28

The insult was listed on the menu as Scotch woodcock. At the beginning of each week, the next seven days' menu was posted on the bulletin board by the entrance to the dayroom. Haystack, the pornographer who lived next to Slick Willy, brought the woodcock to my attention.

"Hey, Harris," he said in his usual loud voice, "you been to Stanford. What the fuck is a woodcock?"

"It's a bird," I said.

"Well, what kinda bird? Is it like a turkey?"

"No, I think it's like a quail."

"Well, it sounds like old Popeye down in the kitchen has finally got his shit together," Haystack blustered. "That dumb cocksucker is gonna serve that wooddick to us on Tuesday."

"Woodcock," I corrected.

"Woodcock, woodcunt, woodhole, whatever you call it, it's up on the menu."

I went up and checked, and sure enough it was. I found it hard to believe when I first read the words. The woodcock is a game bird common to the British Isles, but there it was in black and white.

When Tuesday dinner rolled around, our curiosity was still up. When we lined up at Number 4's door to take our turn in the food parade, the air was full of expectation. I was third man from the front and Jewell was right behind me. We watched across the yard as the Lieutenant opened dinner. He stood on the steps to the administration building with his clipboard and pointed to our door. That meant we could go, and in a rush we hurried down the sidewalk to the chow hall.

When we got our trays and waited in the serving line, visions of game bird died by the hundreds. The main dish was something that looked like creamed tuna, ladled like creamed tuna, and tasted like dog food. Popeye, the chief steward, was standing by the coffee dispenser. Jewell and I stopped next to him on our way toward the dish room.

"Hey, Mr. Popeye," I said.

"Yes," he smiled. Popeye wore a bow tie and looked like a crew-cut five-foot-eight milkman.

"Tell me . . ." I looked down at my tray, and then looked back at his face. "This Scotch woodcock . . ."

"Yes," he beamed.

"Did you shoot it with a howitzer?"

Popeye turned on his heel without an answer, and walked off to inspect the boiled peas. Jewell and I marched over to the counter where dirty trays are stashed, and slid two full ones into the dishwasher.

Out in the yard, what had been a warm day was dying in a stiff, cold wind.

Jewell looked off at the front buildings like he was peering down a well. "You know," he said to me out of the side of his mouth, "we got to do somethin about this shit."

29

I'd been thinking the same thing.

When we found the Squirrel and Eddie Florez standing along the side of Number 3 an hour later, we noticed a lot of others had too. They were fed up.

"We don't got to take all this," Jewell said, "you know that, man."

"For sure," Eddie answered, "but whatta we gonna do?"

"We run a strike on their ass," Jewell snapped back.

"Shit, man, they gonna pull our Good Time if we do that. That's a year and a half."

"Only if we don't work. Man, it ain't no crime not to eat," Jewell argued.

"What kinda strike you call that?"

"A food strike," I said.

The Squirrel broke in. "You know they gonna ship us to the Mission when they find out we're the ones talked it up."

"I been there before," Jewell said.

"So have I," Eddie grinned. "Ain't no big thing. I'm tired of Arizona anyway."

Eddie didn't miss his guess. Three days later, all of us were out of the state. So were Pablo, J.C., Tom Sawyer, the Seagull, Fontera, and Deuce McGuire.

30

The strike opened at the next day's lunch, and we got a break right off. Usually the road crews ate up the hill, but a storm blew in overnight and the blizzard kept us on our bunks in camp all the first day and the next. The road crews were the strike's strength, and worked to solid-up a lot of camp folks. The demands were simple—better food and a real doctor—but the risk of stepping out of the Program was more than some could bear. We lined the barracks doorways and took a good look at everybody that went off to eat. One by one, the Lieutenant pointed. Number 6 was first and they went to eat in a gush. Most of them were Jehovah's Witnesses and didn't truck with rabble-rousing. Number 3 followed, but only eleven went to eat. Number 2 was even tighter than that with eight, and the only ones out of Number 4 were Big Red, the Lizard, Liberace, the Rabbit's clerk, Officer Murphy, and a diabetic who had to eat to stay healthy. All told, 60 percent of Siberia was on strike, and stayed hungry for the next six meals.

The third day started strong and our totals were pushing three-quarters. Then the pressure began. The Rabbit woke up early enough to walk from barracks to barracks before breakfast, telling everyone that anybody who wanted to eat would be given full protection. That brought some stragglers over to our side. Then we went to work. The storm had eased up and the mountain crews were loaded into the trucks without the usual easy movement. The crew bosses were tense and formal, making sure everyone lined up straight. When we got up the road, the crews were told that everyone would be working that day digging a drainage ditch.

"That's mechanics, too," the Crew 2 boss said in my direction.

Tweety Bird issued shovels, and we broke into small groups for the walk up the cut. Tom Sawyer, Pablo, and I were at the back of the crowd. Tom was using his shovel like a cane.

A quarter of a mile up the road, Tom Sawyer stopped. Pablo and I did, too.

"I don't believe we're gonna do this shit," Tom Sawyer said. Before we had a chance to answer, he went on. "I'm not gonna." With that, Tom Sawyer turned and started walking back toward Tweety Bird.

Pablo and I looked at each other.

"What the fuck," he said.

I chewed on my lip and looked off into the wind. It was like sticking my head in a bucket of ice. I looked back at Pablo. "What the fuck," I answered. We caught up with Tom and threw our shovels back into Tweety Bird's truck.

"What're you men doing?" he shrilled. "You can't do that."

"We just did it," I said.

Tweety Bird called the Lieutenant on his radio and the Lieutenant said, "Send em down." Tweety took us back to Siberia in a jeep, and told us to clean out our lockers and report to the Control Room. When we got there, J.C. was waiting.

"They decided you guys needed company," J.C. laughed.

31

On the way out, the four of us were taken to the Rabbit's office. He was behind the desk and didn't ask us to sit. "We gave you men a chance," he began. "This is an honor camp and you men have shown yourselves to be anything but honor-camp material. Officer Tracy will be taking you to the Mission immediately." He paused and looked down at his desk. "Of course," the Rabbit added, "you will lose your Good Time for this."

"Fuck a bunch of Good Time," J.C. said. "It was yours in the first place."

Dick Tracy loaded Tom Sawyer, Pablo, J.C., and me into the Attorney General's Ford and peeled for Texas. I watched the splatters on the windshield. "Here I go again," I said to myself. The words seemed to echo in my head and make my palms itch.

At the New Mexico border, I looked back and saw the storm over Siberia. It was tall and gray, shaped like an Apache heading west.

Part Three
MAXIMUM SECURITY

March 1970-March 1971

Harris, David Victor

height: 6'2''
weight: 175 lbs.
hair: blond
eyes: blue
scars, marks: 2'' left knee
birthdate: 2-28-46
sentence: Federal, 3 years,
          refusal subm. induct.
assignment: C Block, Farm 1,
          Labor 2, Grounds
custody: minimum, medium
eligible parole: Oct. 15,
          1970
parole granted: 3-15-71
good time date: November 3, 1971
release minus 180 days:
          Jan. 16, 1972
maximum release: July 15, 1972

1

As soon as we'd crossed New Mexico, the highway elbowed and headed due east into the Gila Monster badlands. Tracy was silent behind the wheel when we approached a bump to the left of the road. It wasn't much of a rise. Not a mountain, not a hill, just a bump, looking slightly down on the mesquite, and hot bugs dug into the sand on both sides of the state line. The bump was in Texas and the Mission sat on top of the bump, a mile off the highway. I looked across Tracy's shoulders, and wiped my hands on my shirt.

The Mission got its name because of how it looked from the road. The prison has a false front, like a movie set. The Mission part, which faced the public, was topped with a tile roof and a couple of fake bell towers. Behind that front wall, the concrete turned green and was shoebox-shaped. The Spanish architecture broke down into a main building two stories high, housing 780 men in two honor cell blocks, eight dormitories, a maximum security and a disciplinary cell block. There was a furniture factory, an auto shop, a brush factory, a laundry, two small yards, a carpentry shop, an electric shop, a boiler room, and beyond that, a large exercise yard the size of three football fields. All of it was surrounded with a twelve-foot cyclone fence, topped with corkscrew barbed wire. At first glance, I couldn't see the wire. All I saw was the front. It looked like a righteous Mission from the road. For a second, I imagined I was thirteen again, with my family out on vacation from Fresno in our '55 Buick. My dad was behind the wheel: "Oh, David," my mother said from the front seat, "look at that lovely old mission." Then we zipped on past, playing State Capitals and I See Something Red.

Tracy's voice brought me back to the present. He spoke as the Ford wheeled off the main road onto the Mission's mile-long driveway.

"Here's your new home, fellas," he cackled. That's when I noticed the wire and gun towers spun into a web around the church face. "You boys'll learn to act right over here."

We didn't say anything back. We just watched the road slide up the bump like a fuse. On either side were the Mission's farm and dairy, spread out in patches and laced together with a shallow irrigation ditch. As we approached, my eyes fastened on the front tower. It was lighthouse-thick and topped with a glassed-in octagon. From a long way off, the dim glare turned the windows shiny. I couldn't see much but reflection until the Ford turned east again along the institution's front, and stopped at the warning-sign talk box. Then I saw a round head and a 30.06. Dick Tracy leaned out the window and shouted into the speaker.

"Got a carload from Siberia," he said.

The box crackled and spat. "Bring em in," it said. The round head in the tower put his telephone back on the hook and leaned his rifle on the windowsill. As we drove on, the shape came into focus. He was wearing teardrop shades, and his neck hung over his collar. He wore a gray suit, and had his lips clamped together like hamburger buns. Tracy stopped the car at the front steps and told us to get out. I was still staring at the round head in the tower as I stood up. He noticed my gaze. Without shifting his face, the round head lifted his right hand and flipped me the bird.

His middle finger looked like a raw sausage.

2

I felt like I was balanced out on the nose of my life, but I wasn't scared. I had too much concentration for that. Fear distracts the mind, and I was zeroed in on precisely where I was. As soon as Tracy walked us in the front door and through the two barred gates on the other side of the lobby, I switched my radar on. My body wanted to know what being captive here was all about.

I'd grown my radar in Siberia as a matter of self-defense. On the streets, I'd always lived places I belonged and called those places home. I felt safe there and in control. In those days, I had a world my body trusted. It wasn't the same when I belonged to the Attorney General. By the time I reached the Mission, the experience had made me live closer to my skin. The assumption of safety crusted around my existence had flaked away until I felt like I was living out on a platter. There were no props to lean on and no rocks to hide behind. My radar is what I used to deal with this full-blown vulnerability. Like a lizard on a rock, I sensed the hand over my back. My body lost its numbness and I began to know things with my flesh. I hunched my shoulders and read the walls for the feel they broadcast. I counted the particles of danger as they bounced off my back. As the texture of the Mission encountered my own presence, adrenalin pumped into my head. I got high on it, sucking information in through my pores. A lot of pictures flashed on the back of my brain, and they all said I was in a cage much tighter than the one I'd come from. The Mission was not a friendly place. My body felt like the stuffing in a concrete sandwich. There were no signs of myself anywhere I looked.

I didn't need to tell anyone else how I felt. J.C., Tom Sawyer, and Pablo were all doing the same thing. All of our eyes looked vacant, like our lives had run off into our skin. My hands were cold and wet.

Tracy told us to sit on the chairs outside the records office while he delivered our files. We were in a long linoleum hallway that ran on past our seats to another gate with an electric lock. J.C. nudged my elbow.

"This is just the caseworkers' offices and all that shit," he said. "Convict territory don't begin until that Control Room there on the other side of the gate."

I lit a Camel and gave one to Pablo. We waited for Tracy with our feet up on the boxes of property we'd brought along. Tracy was back in five minutes with another gray suit. At that point, we were officially in the Mission, and the last trace of Siberia went back out the hallway the way he'd come. None of us watched

Tracy leave. As far as we were concerned, he was already somewhere else.

The new cop led us down to the next gate and signaled the Control Room to buzz it open. Once we were all through, our convoy took a hard right onto the Mission's main thoroughfare, a hallway with a twenty-foot ceiling and polished cement floors. The walls were thirty feet apart, and painted the color of gangrene. We walked as far as a metal door halfway to the end of the hall. The cop opened it with his key and introduced us to the Basement. Joe Friday was on duty at the time. He locked the door behind us.

Joe Friday looked at me like I was a pound of ground round. "What's your name and number?" he snapped.

"Harris," I said. "4697."

He asked J.C., Tom Sawyer, and Pablo the same question. Then he told us to stack our boxes of property. "You'll get em back when they put you in population," Friday added. The next step was a frisk, followed by the removal of our belts and shoelaces. "Don't want none of you hangin yourselves back there," he grinned. Then Friday led us through another gate, past two lines of cells, and through a door to our rooms for the duration. There was no electric light in any of the cells we were assigned. Just a shitter, a bunk with steel plates for springs, a mattress, and a blanket. Joe Friday gave each of us a toothbrush and walked back to his post.

My cell's window was thick glass fitted into iron frames. It looked out through wire mesh onto the fence and the gun tower past that. I couldn't see the round head from my cell.

That night, I made the mistake of leaving the window cracked open. I woke up with an inch of fine sand in the creases of my blanket. The sounds of morning were moving along the concrete like cans scattering in an alley.

3

Down in the Basement, I learned time has a body, too. It's a thing of substance. Being locked up alone with it, I began to see time as a solid mass I burrowed in and carved into shapes. I stalked my cage from one end to the other, shoveling through moments, pushing days aside in my wake. The time I would spend there was my only Basement resource. I tried to use it as best I could.

Aside from pacing, I did a lot of push-ups and drank a lot of water. In between, I lay on my bunk staring at the wall and used my imagination to paste odd chunks of hours into scenes pleasing to my mind. I projected them on the concrete surface two feet away. The scripts varied, but in all of them I was the center of the situation, engaging in acts that reverberated throughout the cosmos. My favorite was when I played for UCLA in the NCAA finals and won the game with a back-handed stuff shot. I basked in the roar of the crowd. All of the fantasies were medicine for a self infected with the reality of counting little and controlling even less. I learned to keep myself company and tame my deprived senses with bits of fiction and small doses of self-induced hallucination.

The only interruptions were the meal tray that came under the door three times a day, and Joe Friday to count every so often. When I'd picked through the meal, I slid the tray out in the hall and returned to my nine-by-seven day.

It was a simple life, full of not much more than I could invent. Stripped of stuff to stack around me, I learned to manufacture the ingredients necessary to an existence. I built a life out of my head and the little bit of body that was still mine to use. The only other option was learning to live like a chair leg, and that was no option at all. I survived because I did what I had to. Even so, it never stopped being lonely and cold.

When I needed reassurance, I talked to J.C. or Pablo. The conversation involved shouting out the front of my cell and then turning my head to listen. None of us could see the others, but they lived on in my ears until I saw their faces again. We didn't have much to say after a while, but any news was passed on in a hurry. On the second day, J.C. said he heard Curly shouting from the block on the other side of the door.

"Outta sight," I said. "Anybody else?"

"He said there's all kinds of folks from Siberia up there with him," J.C.'s voice answered.

A lot of old friends were within shouting distance, but it was five more days until we made the acquaintance of anyone who'd been at the Mission before we got there.

His name was Ferdinand Pudge and he had an exceptional presence.

4

Everybody called him Pudgy for short. After he hit the Basement, we had a lot to watch for a while. The quiet days were suddenly full of interruption.

Pudgy was a little, low rider from the San Fernando Valley, built like a cross between Sonny Liston and a fireplug. He stood all of five foot seven and weighed better than two hundred pounds. Pudgy was a car thief and, unlike most in his profession, not in the habit of taking a whole lot of shit. It was Pudgy's attitude that brought him down to visit us in the Basement.

It all began in the same front hallway we'd been led into by Dick Tracy. Pudgy was just cruising up to see his caseworker when he was approached by John Wayne. John Wayne was the captain, boss cop at the Mission and in the habit of not taking a lot of shit himself. He expected convicts to jump when he said so. The captain saw the hair starting to sneak over Pudge's ears.

"You, Pudge," John Wayne growled, "come over here."

Pudgy walked over and looked up at John Wayne. As captain, he wore a blue suit and a western buckle to hold his pants up and shirt down.

"Yah?" Pudgy said.

"You need a haircut," John Wayne ordered. "I want you to report back here in an hour, and stop at the barber on the way." The captain said all his words without showing his teeth. He kept his lips pressed together like two rulers, so the sound seemed to burst from the side of his neck.

His manner was just part of what made John Wayne fearsome. To go with it, he had a six-foot-three slab to live inside of, with a chest like an oil drum. The captain was lobster-skinned, with tiny veins popping up all along the crease in his nose. On top of all that meat, John Wayne had a record, which was more fearsome than anything else.

Before he came to the Mission, the captain had been a lieutenant somewhere in Indiana. There he'd paralyzed a man from the waist down. John Wayne was whipping on him one day, and just whipped a little too hard. He told the inquiry afterward that it was a matter of self-defense. Then he was moved to the Mission with a promotion, and a right hand that hit like a bazooka. John Wayne was a scary fella, but it didn't seem to affect Pudgy in the least.

Pudge walked into John Wayne's office in an hour and told him to stick his haircut up his ass. Not a whole lot of folks talked to the captain that way, and according to the version Pudgy told, John Wayne consumed thirty seconds of silence admitting to himself that it happened. Two minutes later, Pudgy came to the Basement under heavy escort. Joe Friday put him in the cell at the far end.

As far as Pudge was concerned, the fight had just begun. The first time he felt the urge, he squatted in the corner and crapped a small pile of crap. Pudge saved it until Joe Friday came along the cell fronts to count. Then Pudge threw the turds at Friday's head. To make his point as strongly as he could, Pudgy rattled his cell door all night. Needless to say, we were all awake in time to hear him lob a handful of oatmeal at the morning shift's chest.

The morning shift ran and got John Wayne.

"What're you gonna do when that big red-necked son of a bitch gets here?" I shouted down to Pudge.

"Get a little exercise," he said.

He got it in no uncertain terms. Five minutes later, John Wayne stood in front of Pudgy's cell with his hands on his hips.

"Look, Pudge," John Wayne warned, "if you don't learn how to behave yourself real quick, I'm gonna have to come in there and whip on ya."

"Well, Captain," Pudge said, "you got the key to the door. Anytime you want to open it, you just go ahead and do it to your heart's content." Pudgy said the words from the back wall of his cell, strung tight like a cat on the pounce.

"I'll be back," John Wayne promised.

An hour later, he returned and brought a few friends along to help. The captain had six cops with him, and they all had riot gear. John Wayne was in his shirt-sleeves.

"Open Number 24," he called to Joe Friday.

Joe Friday pulled the iron lever and Number 24 came open with a clank. It was clear from the look on his face that the captain figured to bounce Pudgy off the wall a few times, and that'd be that. Pudge figured different. He came off the back wall with two quick jumps and put a left just above John Wayne's pure-brass, God-Bless-America belt buckle. Pudge followed with a right that pried the captain's lip up so his gold eye-teeth showed, and put him on his ass in the corner of the hallway. Then the six cops took over and split the skin over Pudgy's eye with a nightstick. Pudge ended up on his face and unconscious in Number 24.

Pudge was back at it as soon as he came to. He and John Wayne repeated the same scene once a day for the next six days. It got to be a regular form of entertainment for us all. On the sixth day, Pudgy closed John Wayne's eye with a left hook. The captain flew against the door to Number 8 and Joe Friday grabbed Pudge from behind. Then the Wop Cop ran up and put his foot straight on Pudgy's nuts. When Pudge went to his knees, the Wop Cop kicked him again.

Pudgy was puking off and on, all night long. We called Joe Friday and told him we had a sick man, but he laughed.

"The only medicine that man needs is a haircut," Friday scoffed.

The whole affair seemed to make its point on Ferdinand Pudge. He spent his evening meditating with his head stuck over the shitter and dinner splashing onto his pants. The morning of the seventh day, Pudge changed strategies.

So did the captain. John Wayne returned to the Basement with a bandage on the side of his head. "Look, Pudge," he began, "I'm willing to forget everything that's happened here. I'll forget you assaulted an officer. I'll forget all the other charges. All you got to do is get a haircut."

In an hour, Pudgy left the Basement. He went through the doors, and we could hear the far gate bang open and shut as he made it to the hallway. Pudge walked straight to the barbershop and sat in the chair. He told the barber to shave his head and the barber did just as he was told.

Pudgy was right when he said the haircut made him look like a new man, but it didn't solve his problem with John Wayne. The Mission's regulations forbid shaved heads, too. Pudgy got the barber to polish his dome a little with a towel, and went bebopping out into the hall. The first person he saw was John Wayne.

The first thing John Wayne saw was Pudgy's head. It glistened. "What the . . ." he roared. He never finished his statement. Pudgy had seized the initiative. While the captain stood flatfooted with his mouth open, Pudgy ran toward him, jumped in the air, threw his legs around the captain's waist and his arms around his shoulders. Then Pudgy kissed John Wayne full on the lips. Before the captain could react, Pudgy jumped off and skipped down the hallway. John Wayne started to yell after him, but thought better of it and walked back to his office. He stayed there the rest of the day.

After that, no one fucked with Pudgy. Even John Wayne stayed off his case, which is more than the rest of us could say.

The rest of us stayed in the Basement for another fifteen days and watched the sun come up in the morning and leave at night. I numbered the days by making scratches in the paint above my shitter with a broken pencil.

5

There weren't any holidays in the Basement, but every now and then we got a special treat. It came in the form of cigarettes delivered through a smuggle known as the Nicotine Railway, a convict invention of the first magnitude.

J.C. was in the cell to my left, and closest to the door. As such, he was snatch man and a key link in the smuggle. The cigarettes started in the front half of the block, on the other side of the door. Curly gave the Cleaner five loose Camels when Joe Friday opened the Cleaner's door so he could sweep the hall. As the Cleaner worked his broom past our door, he swept the smokes under its edge with a pack of matches. From there on, the action was all J.C.'s.

J.C. took the slip off his mattress and fished, casting the cotton cover over the Camels. When he had them all under the cloth, he reeled the mattress cover back in like a net. Then he plucked out the cigarettes and made a second cast for the fire. One by one, J.C. flipped the catch down the block until we were all supplied. I lit mine right away and passed the matches on. The smoke slipped into my lungs like a tongue. I lay back and felt like my own man until the butt got so short it burned my fingers.

After a while, I got so I depended on Nicotine Railway cigarettes to shore up my self-respect the way no ordinary cigarette ever could. The best part about it was that it wasn't supposed to happen. It was proof we did exist after all.

6

After our second week down in the Basement, the Mission slowly began to digest our numbers and funnel us toward the rest of the population. For openers, we were each taken to see our caseworker. I was the first to go. Joe Friday opened my door and walked me up to the office. I counted my steps along the cement floor and marveled at all the space out in the hall.

The meeting started out small. Just me, Errol Flynn, and the desk. Errol Flynn was the chief caseworker. Thanks to his mustache, Errol Flynn was handsome. The brush covered his slight hairlip and gave him a strong smile. Flynn spoke clearly and with frosting. He made the Mission sound like a bowl of milk punch run by retired cub scouts. There was a brace of papers on the desk. The caseworker opened the conversation by asking me to fill them out.

I took fifteen minutes to do it. I could have been quicker but I wanted to stretch the time. It was nice to be out of the Basement. Flynn's office had a deep rug and pictures of the Attorney General on the wall. The Attorney General had a chin like a sea elephant. When I finally finished, Errol Flynn spoke up.

"You're a new inmate here," he said, "and we like to meet with each newcomer and let him know how we run things here."

"I've got some idea already," I responded.

Errol Flynn continued like he hadn't heard me.

"When the warden decides to put you out in the population, you'll be assigned quarters and a job. Work call is 7:30. As long as you go to work and stay out of trouble, you'll get seven days a month Good Time. If you look at the Time Card here, you'll see it's already figured in. November of 1971. You'll go to the Parole Board again this year in October. You've got a lot of disciplinary reports now, but if you keep your nose clean, there's a good chance you'll get a favorable hearing. Just do the number we've given you and you'll get along. We won't hold what you did at Siberia against you. It's a new ball game here, and I hope we get to be friends. Just work toward that meeting with the board, and I'm sure we will. Any questions?" he asked.

I had a few.

"When do we get out of the Basement?" I wanted to know.

"You'll be moved from the Disciplinary Section when the warden decides you are ready to go out into population." Errol Flynn enunciated Disciplinary Section slowly, so I would learn the right name from the start. "I'm sure it will be soon. How long have you been down there?"

"Two weeks," I answered.

The words had a little echo in my head and I was having trouble staying in the conversation. Flynn's office window looked out over a brown lawn with a tree in the middle. The winds had died off, and the air outside was quiet and butter colored. Seven sparrows were hopping around the branches. Errol Flynn's voice sounded far away.

"Well, it won't be much longer," he assured me. "The warden's a busy man, but I'm sure he'll move you as soon as he gets the forms."

I had one more question. I pulled back from the sparrows and looked at Flynn head on.

"Can you explain to me just what I'm doing in Texas? My family's in California and they have to come fifteen hundred miles to visit me. I thought the law said a prisoner is supposed to be kept in the prison closest to his family."

"It does," Flynn responded. "Do you want a transfer?"

"For sure," I said.

Errol Flynn handed me another form. "Fill out this transfer request, and I'll submit it to the warden. When he approves it, you'll be on your way to California."

I picked up the pencil in front of me. "Is the warden going to approve it?" I asked.

"That's up to the warden," Errol Flynn answered. "But in a case like yours, with family and all, I'm sure he'll seriously consider it. We don't like to see men lose their ties with their families."

I filled out the form and got ready to go back to the Basement. While I was in the middle of a last look at the birds, the door opened without a knock, and John Wayne came into the office with Warden Gruff.

7

Warden Gruff scared me right off, and in a way John Wayne never did. John Wayne might bruise you, but he couldn't get inside your head like the warden. Gruff had a way of finding your hopes and squeezing them as hard as he could. It was a knack he'd developed over the years, and a sure sign he had his act well in hand. I'd dealt with a lot of cops by the time I got to the warden, and hadn't run into any that I couldn't shuck and jive, slide around, or handle to my advantage face to face. Warden Gruff broke my string. He had me wanting something, and that was all the advantage he needed. Fortunately, he got promoted shortly after I reached population, but he was around long enough to find my number and step on it. He was fat and wore glasses with black plastic rims. His mouth always had a smile at its edges and a cigar right in the middle. The cigar hung on his teeth like a body on a picket fence.

We had a short conversation.

"Warden," I said, as soon as he stopped in the doorway, "Mr. Flynn and I've just been talking about a transfer."

"You don't like it here?"

"Well," I said, "I've got a family in California and I want to be closer to them. We've got a young child, and I'd get to see a lot more of him if I were in California."

The warden's face softened. "How old is he?"

"Oh . . ." I was surprised he'd asked. Unwittingly, I loosened my mind and fell into thinking about my boy. "He's four months," I bragged.

"You miss him?"

I did and I made the mistake of telling Warden Gruff. "Sure do," I said.

"Tough shit," he answered.

Warden Gruff's smile never changed as he reached over Errol Flynn's desk and grabbed my fresh transfer request. He wadded it up and dropped it in the wastebasket on his way out. John Wayne told Flynn he'd send Friday up to take me back, and followed the warden.

Back in the Basement, it was a day just like the one before and the one after. The cell was full of shadows and little puddles of light. I sat on my bunk and fiddled with my time. To warm up, I molded it into a horse. Then I took the whole day and tried to make it into Faro's house on Kearney Street. Faro was a woman I knew when I was traveling the West Coast for the Resistance. She lived on the third floor, and I let myself in with the key she kept in the mailbox. I remember the light in her bedroom like the one in my cell. Not really a light, just the leavings of one. Just enough light to know where everything is, but little enough so that you have to squint to make sure. I had Faro in between the sheets three or four times, and then Joe Friday came by with dinner. He slid the tray under the gate, and all the time I'd stacked fell down and scattered on the floor. I tried to build it back, but I never could get it to fit in one piece again.

After I gave up, I ate the pork, and slid the rest with the tray back into the hall. I used my thumbnail to pick my teeth, and wanted to tie up the warden in

August and drown him in September. I tried to mold the feeling into a shape, but there wasn't enough of the day left. I couldn't make much out of time in the dark. When it got dark, I just let time sit on me like a weight, and cried so no one would hear me.

8

I saw Warden Gruff twice after that.

The first time was right after we changed neighborhoods. When we'd all finished seeing Errol Flynn, we moved another rung up the ladder and got cells on the front side of the door. It was the same seven-by-nine, twenty-four hours a day, but we got light and cigarettes. The light was a comfort and the cigarettes were like money in the bank. We were all glad to move. In the last few days, the Basement had become a specially hard place to live.

Mostly it was because of the guy who ate razor blades. We didn't even know his name. He came down the day we moved, and spoke no English. He hardly spoke any Mexican either. He mostly did two things. Either he sat on the shitter and screamed, or he sat on his bunk and looked at his feet. I couldn't figure him out until the Wasp explained. The Wasp lived up in the front of the Basement and got to mop the hall once a day. He'd been down in the Basement longest, so the mopping job was his by seniority. He knew the guy who ate razor blades.

"He's crazy," the Wasp explained. "He comes down here a lot. This time the motherfucker ate some more blades. He'd done it before too. The first time he did it, you know, they cut him open and took em out. But he's done it so much, now they just send him down with a dose of Ex-Lax. It'll be all right as soon as he shits em out."

We could hear him on the other side of the door. He started with a low moan. Then the moans started coming in bursts until they climbed into a scream, a scream with wings on it that rattled around the Basement like a trapped bird. The scream had a high pitch that chewed at my brain until I thought it would leak out my ears. The screaming lasted twenty minutes, five or six times a day. Between sounds, J.C., Pablo, Tom Sawyer, and I renewed our acquaintance with Curly. All the rest of the folks from Siberia were out in population already, but he stayed behind. Down in the Basement, he, Joe, and the Wasp had become regular features. Curly had refused to work from his first day at the Mission, four months before, and so had Joe. The Wasp, on the other hand, would've been glad to take a job out with everybody else, but the captain wouldn't let him.

9

The Wasp was a dope fiend. When you're one of those, it's hard to be anything else at the same time, so there's not much to tell about the Wasp except he shot dope and got arrested. The way he told the story, the Wasp should never have been busted.

"I didn't have to," he said near the end of March. He was leaning on his mop in front of my cell door. "If only my partners had held their shit. But you can't trust no junky. They're all fools. Me and Julio and this friend of his had all gone to Martinez's place. We all wanted to shoot some good stuff and Martinez's was the best. He had a shooting gallery in the back of his pad. And it wasn't like most of the others. Martinez sold righteous dope. Nice big old fluffy white shit. Mixed a hell of a speedball, too. It was good stuff. Almost too good. I got hungry for it, and after we all fixed the first time, right away I paid Martinez to go around again. Just a taste to put me on the top, I told Julio, but he couldn't give a shit. He was on the nod and didn't say nothin. As soon as I got that motherfuckin second load in my vein, I knew right away I was fucked up. I went out cold, and when Martinez comes back from stashin the cash, he thinks I'm dead. He grabs Julio and his friend and tells em I OD'd. 'He's dead,' Martinez says. 'You got to get this body outta my pad.' Julio and his friend are all fucked up, but Martinez don't give em no choice. He whipped out a piece, and tells em to move it. At least that's what Julio said later.

"They stagger around and carry me out to the trunk of Julio's Mercury. That gets me off Martinez's back, but it don't solve Julio's problem. He's got a body on his hands and don't know what to do with it. 'Take him to the cemetery,' his friend says. So about three in the morning they sneak into a graveyard. Fuckin Julio almost broke his leg fallin in a fresh hole. 'Fuck it,' he says, and he leaves me. He and his fuckin friend left me in the grave Julio'd fallen in, and took off. The night watchman found my body and called the cops. When they got there, I was just comin back. I looked up outta my grave, still half on the nod, and there ain't nothin but cops all around me. They went through my clothes and I still had a bag of stuff in my jacket, so I get this nickel. Just cause that fuckin Julio can't hold his mud."

"What'd you do to Julio?" I asked.

The Wasp looked down the hall to make sure Joe Friday wasn't back from the office yet before he continued. "Oh, I forgive him," the Wasp said. "He felt bad and righteously thought I was dead. That ain't shit, but what am I gonna do? I been knowin Julio since we was kids."

"You ever see him now?"

"Sure. He visits me once a month. That's how I got down here. I don't mean it was Julio's fault," the Wasp added. "The Pig was the one that did it to me. You don't know the Pig yet, but you'll see him when you get out in the hallways. That's one snitchin motherfucker.

"It all started when Julio came on a visit. He'd visit maybe once every two weeks, and he'd bring me stuff. Julio'd have it all done up in a balloon, the kind kids have at birthday parties. When the cop out in the visiting wasn't lookin, I'd swallow it. They can't search your guts, so I come through shakedown clean and slick every time. Then I'd go back to my cell and puke the balloon up. That balloon'd bob in my shitter, and I'd stay noddin till Julio came back. They had me livin on the honor block I was such a good boy. I kept the stuff to myself and Hot Rod, cause he was a homey. I didn't even want the Rod in on it, but he had the outfit. Me and him'd shoot up out in the warehouse where he stashed his fit.

"One day we came out so loaded we couldn't see straight, and run into the Pig. Just by lookin he knows we're fucked up, and he goes to the lieutenant and gives us up. I saw em comin and flushed my stuff, but they got me for usin. I didn't plead to nothin, but they locked me up in the hospital cell and shut the water to the shitter off. I didn't know they'd shut it off, so I just go over to take a piss. When I finish, the cops come back in and took a sample out of the bowl. I tried to flush it, but it wouldn't go. They sent my piss to the chemist, and tell me I'm usin heroin.

" 'I don't use dope no more,' I told em, but they never believed me. I been down here ever since. If they put me back out in population, I'm going kill the Pig. The captain knows that. That's why I'm gonna stay down here for as long as I got left."

The Wasp told his story a lot. He'd forget who he'd told and who he hadn't, so we all got to hear a second and third time. The second time, Warden Gruff came through right in the middle.

We heard him coming. Opening and closing two locked gates and a door is a dead giveaway. He was on an inspection tour. The warden walked along in his Florsheims and looked into each cell. He had the same smile and the same cigar as he'd had before. He stopped at my gate.

"How's our little revolutionary?" he asked.

"Lookin for a new home," I said.

Gruff laughed and walked to the next cell. When he got to J.C.'s, J.C. started telling him why we should get out of the Basement. He listened for a minute, and then walked off while J.C. was in the middle of a sentence. We heard him leave with two clanks and a thud.

"That's one hard-assed motherfucker," J.C. sighed.

10

The second time I saw Warden Gruff was April 2. I wasn't too sure, but I couldn't have been off by more than a day. J.C. and Pablo'd gone into population two days before and I figured I was next. I was right. Before I left, the warden came back to my cell.

"I'm gonna let you into population," he said, "but I want you to understand something first. I looked at your jacket and you've been making trouble regularly. I don't like that. I'd like to let the captain string you up by your nuts, but that's not prison policy. Even so, comrade, you listen to me and listen good. I'm only gonna tell you once. The second time, I'll have your ass in the last cage on the line. If you even think about doin any of the shit you did in the last place you were at, you're gonna spend the rest of your time back with the crazy man." Gruff pulled his cigar out, and pointed at the back door. Then he turned on his heel and left.

I got moved up to Maximum Security after the four o'clock count.

When Friday opened my door, I said good-by to Curly, Joe, and Tom Sawyer. Tom had decided to go Curly's route and quit work. Then I said good-by to the Wasp.

"Hey," the Wasp said, as I carried my box of property out of the cell, "if you see a dude named Jimmy from San Antone, tell him to do me a favor. I'm hurtin. He'll know what you mean."

Joe Friday walked me up the steel stairs just outside the gate and before the door. At the top, we turned left after he unlocked the gate leading to a block of twenty-four cells, twelve on each side of the hallway. I left my box in Number 24, and Friday let me out the door into the upstairs hall. I headed straight for the yard.

It was still light outside. The sun was on its way down and had turned the sky into spoiled milk. It was broken into curds and stretching as far as I could see. J.C. and Jewell were out watching the handball games when I came down the steps. They saw me and ran over.

"All right." Jewell laughed and slapped my hand. "They finally let you come out here with us good folks, huh?"

"Shit," I said, pulling the word out like taffy. I looked at all the open space over the wall and felt the cramp in my shoulders begin to loosen.

"Before I forget," I remembered, "do you know someone named Jimmy from San Antone? I got a message for him."

"You're a little late," J.C. answered. "He's been in the hospital for the last week. Got into it with the Brown Bomber."

"The who?"

"The Brown Bomber. See that big old stringy dude by the weight pile?"

I looked and saw a six-foot-five convict standing bare-chested by the barbells. He had hair the color of rusted wire.

"That's him," J.C. continued. "Jimmy ain't sayin who did it, but a friend of mine from Duke City saw it. The Bomber ate his ass up."

I watched the Bomber lean over and jerk the bar up as he sucked great masses of air into his chest.

11

As time passed, I got to know the Bomber as well as anyone. The Brown Bomber was my neighbor. He lived in Number 21 and I in Number 24, so we couldn't see each other most of the time we talked. We were on the same side of the hall, but I got to know his face in the yard. He had a scar that started at the lower side of his right eyelid and ran straight as Highway 99 into his shirt collar. The Bomber said he got it in the Korean War and I believed him.

He told me the story in snatches, out of his cell front and waiting in line for dinner. The Bomber remembered as far back as when he was twelve. He forgot everything before he was sent to the orphans' home. A year later, he ran off and stayed loose for a month. When the Young Bomber was caught, the Young Bomber got sent to reform school. It took another two years before he busted out of there. The Bomber then made his way to San Francisco and enlisted in the Marine Corps by lying about his age. After boot camp the Bomber was sixteen, and on his way to join the First Marines around a reservoir near the Chinese border. It was cold enough to freeze the hair off your ass, and the marines had fought all the way from Inchon. They were tired and needed men, but they all figured they'd just about licked the dinks anyway.

When he reached his company, the captain sent the Young Bomber out on the perimeter and the sergeant put him in a hole with a guy named Mackinathahaway, or something like that. The Bomber never did quite catch his name. They were both chattering so hard from the cold that it was hard to talk. It was easier to blow on your mittens. The Young Bomber and whatever his name was did just that for the next two hours. Then the dinks licked back.

They came from everywhere—out of all the ridges and every little crack in the mountains. The Young Bomber looked up, and whatever-his-name-was didn't have a front half to his face anymore. A .30-caliber machine gun was the obvious reason. The Bomber blew it up with a grenade, but it didn't make much difference. The sergeant brought two .50s up but that didn't, either. The guns made a lot of noise, but good God, there were more dinks fifty yards away than the Young Bomber ever thought existed in the whole world. They were moving fast and headed due south. The marines picked up on their plans real quick, and whoever was left decided to go south before the dinks closed the

road. The Young Bomber carried his old foxhole partner for three miles until a medic told him he was dead.

As the company made their retreat, the Bomber was
sent to the head of the column with the point patrol.
He got close to a guy named Luigi from Seattle. The
first night heading south, their outfit got hit with artil-
lery and the Young Bomber lost his youth. Huddled
in an icy ditch, he shit his pants. He had nothing to
change into and Luigi started calling him the Brown
Bomber. By the time they'd covered fifty more miles
of mud, bodies, and dead trucks, it was the only name
he had.

After those fifty miles, the company came to a dead
end. The road went into a deep cut in the mountains,
and the dinks were crawling all over the top of the cut.
To get through, the marines had to let the dinks shoot
at them for three and a half miles. At the same time,
intelligence said four or five divisions were just twenty
miles north and coming quick. The lieutenant was the
only live officer anyone could find. He said to get
everybody on the trucks and run through it. The
lieutenant was in the back of the first truck, laid out in
the bed. He'd had his arm blown off just an hour before. The medic said he'd stopped the bleeding, and
the lieutenant led the convoy into the pass. He died
a hundred yards down the road, and the truck made it
another twenty feet before the dinks finished it with a
mortar round.

The sergeant said they had to take the ridge, and
sent the Brown Bomber's squad to eliminate the closest
machine gun. The Bomber and Luigi made it all the
way to the gun. Luigi tossed a grenade in the gun pit,
and they all jumped in. The Bomber stuck the only
live dink, and things looked a lot better until fifty dinks

showed up in a bunch. A grenade ground the bottom half of Luigi into dog food. The Bomber was fifteen feet away, and the blast knocked him cold.

When the Brown Bomber woke up, he'd taken a couple of pieces of shrapnel and a trip forty miles east to where the dinks had a prisoner-of-war camp. The Brown Bomber was there for two more months until he ran off.

In the meantime, he picked up the scar. A guard at the POW camp gave it to him on the second day he was there. The Bomber was singled out for not having the right attitude and the boss dink marked him. The guard used a bayonet to do the job. The Brown Bomber almost died of blood poisoning from it. When he finally recovered, the Bomber strangled a guard and headed south.

Back behind American lines, the front had stabilized. After intelligence got through with him, the Bomber was sent to a company doing night patrols. Their job was to pick up squads of dinks who were trying to infiltrate. It was a good company, and they caught a lot of dinks. They had a ritual they went through with the captives. The Brown Bomber told me about it three days after I'd moved onto the block. We were standing next to each other waiting for our turn to walk past the steam table to get our oatmeal and French toast.

"It all depended on how many we took," he explained. "If we just took one, we'd shoot him. If we got more than that, we'd line em up in a row. Then this guy from Tennessee would come down the row with a machete. He'd take off every head but the last dink. I'd cut the nuts off the dead ones and stuff a set in each mouth. Then we'd put the heads in a gunnysack, and send the live one back to the dink lines with the bag."

The Brown Bomber wanted to stay in the marines after the war, but the corps retired him. He fucked around for a while, and ended up shooting the shit out of an FBI man in the course of ripping off a bank in Tucson. Before his case was finished, the Bomber had thirty years to do. When we met, he already had ten of them under his belt. The Bomber didn't mess much with other folks, but Jimmy from San Antone should never have run his head at him the way he did. The Bomber just wasn't the kind to put up with it. Jimmy was lucky to get off with a broken arm.

The Brown Bomber and I did most of our talking after I got back to my cell from work. I was usually sweaty and covered with a thin layer of silt. The whole block was locked in from 4 to 5:30, and I started the wait by splashing water on my face from the sink. Then I'd settle down in my folding chair next to the bars, and catch up on the Bomber's story. He was just three doors down. On the books, our home was called Maximum Security, but was better known as the Birdcage. The Brown Bomber and I lived there with twenty-two others.

12

Our block got the name Birdcage because of all the birds who lived there. Fourteen cells' worth, to be exact.

The boss bird was called Queen Bee. "A pussy with a stinger," is how she was explained out in the yard. She was in Number 4, right down by the police station. The cell block ended at a locked gate, and eight feet past it was a solid, locked door. Between the two, and next to the cell levers, was a folding chair. The folding chair was the police station. Number 4 was catty-corner from it, and firmly in the cop's line of sight. The cop used to lie up there in the evenings and watch Queen Bee shave her legs at the sink.

All the birds lived close to the gate to make watching easier. They were in Maximum Security by virtue of being outrageous. As a rule, they wore silk panties and were into perfume and plucked brows. All of that was against the rules, but that didn't stop any of the birds. It didn't even cross Queen Bee's mind; she'd been other things, but she liked being a bird best.

Queen Bee started life as Juan Gutierrez, a Golden Gloves champion in Juárez. She lost in the semifinals of the Mexican Nationals and went across the border to look around and maybe fight if she could. The Border Patrol picked Queen Bee up on her second day across. During the last eight years, she'd done four sentences, and had three more years she was working on when I knew her.

In her administrative jacket, Queen Bee was a homo-
sexual. On various corners of the yard, she was called
stuff, punk, donut, sissie, and one fine motherfucker.
But everybody called her Queen Bee to her face. She
liked it that way, and it was widely known that Queen
Bee wasn't the kind of person to be on the wrong side
of. When she first came to the Mission, there were six
Apaches from Laredo who hadn't heard. They made
two very dangerous mistakes.

Queen Bee was just breaking in as a bird then. The
cops still let her live in a dormitory. Queen Bee and
Laurace Scudder lived bunk by bunk in One West.
She hadn't started to paint her mole or shave the hair
on her asshole yet, but Queen Bee was already doing it
the way she liked best. The Apaches couldn't help but
notice, and came up one day to announce they were
going to fuck her. Queen Bee told the Apaches that she
fucked who she wanted and she didn't want them.
Their first mistake was not stopping there.

Their second mistake was cornering Queen Bee in
the shitters when she went down to take a piss. They
all barely lived to regret it. Queen Bee grabbed a mop
bucket and split open the two closest heads. The rest
grabbed their friends and ran off. Queen Bee didn't
forget. The next day she caught one of the others out
on the handball courts and knocked his eyelid off with
a right hook. The captain sent her to the Basement for
it, but when she got out, she waited a week for one of
the others, caught him alone behind the laundry, and
put a ball peen hammer through the back of his skull.

The Apaches never forgot Queen Bee. None of the
rest of us did, either. We all treated her like a fine lady,
and we were right.

She was a fine married lady to be exact. Queen Bee
was married three or four different times while I knew

her. She was knee-deep in romance with Horatio Alger when I reached population. They hung around together outside the Catholic chapel after 7:30 count. From then until 9 we were allowed out of our cells for evening recreation. That meant one of the small yards, the hobby shop, or walking in the hallway. The chapel was upstairs across from the Birdcage door. All of the birds fucked there when it was empty in the evenings, or in the laundry during the day. While the others stood point, one couple would get in back of the altar and slide it in and out.

On Monday nights, Queen Bee would put on her best silk panties, brush her mole, and Horatio'd take her out in the little yard by the warehouse where the boxing matches were shown on Mexican TV. When they arrived, a hundred men were sucked up around the tube, waiting for the preliminaries. Queen Bee walked like her hips were water, and Horatio smiled like he was the slickest son of a bitch that ever chanced through Texas.

He wasn't.

13

Horatio Alger wasn't even close. His biggest accomplishments were a few burglaries and a little hot paper in Oklahoma City, but he loved Queen Bee like the left eye loves the right. That was Horatio's downfall. Whenever Queen Bee threatened divorce, Horatio would lose his head and beg her to stay. His weakness meant Queen Bee could get anything she wanted from Horatio. She proceeded to take everything he had.

"If you love me," Queen Bee told Horatio, "you give me presents. If you don't, I guess you no love me no more."

Horatio lavished her with gifts. He gave Queen Bee $50 worth of commissary every month. That's a lot of candy and cigarettes, especially since each of us was only allowed to draw $25 worth. That meant Horatio had to steal, gamble, or get a loan for $25 a month more, plus the cost of his own smokes and razor blades. Mostly he borrowed. That's what hurt him.

The source of Horatio's funds was the loan sharks. There were six of them in the Mission, and they liked to collect. During the first week of June, they liked to collect so hard that Horatio came within an inch of bleeding a whole lot. He went to the lieutenant for protection, and was sent to deadlock in the Birdcage, where his meals were brought in. Out in the hallway Horatio owed better than $100, but safe in the block he was out of debt. Alger was just down and across the hall from Queen Bee. She consoled him and blew kisses until the next commissary day. Then she started in with a young redneck from Pecos. It broke Horatio's heart.

For two days he begged her to come back to him, but he was begging with empty hands. The young redneck had left a hickey on Queen Bee's neck, and she showed it to Horatio every time he tried to talk to her. It all finally got to Horatio on the ninth of June.

"Queen Bee," he shouted across the hall, "you wronged me. You took all my money and then left me for trash that'd never been fifteen miles from the Pecos River before he come to the penitentiary. I treated you good, Queen Bee," he moaned. "I loved you with all my heart."

Then Horatio drank two quarts of mosquito repellent. It didn't kill him, but it sure made him puke and shit in his pants. Joe Friday found him ten minutes after he'd swallowed the bug juice. Horatio screamed and moaned all the way to the hospital to have his stomach pumped. After that, Queen Bee wouldn't even answer his calls. Horatio finally got a transfer to Terminal Island. Fair Deal, the loan shark, spent two weeks in the Basement right after Horatio left. Queen Bee stayed in the Birdcage where she'd started, and where she was boss bird.

To get to the Birdcage, we all had to be searched at the hallway door. Queen Bee was usually in her cell when I got through the shakedown. On occasion, she offered me cookies.

"You work hard," she'd say, "must be hungry." I took the cookies every time. If I asked, she'd press my visiting clothes and get me new T-shirts.

One afternoon before she split from Horatio, she and I had our only substantial conversation. I had the afternoon off to visit the dentist, and when I was finished I spent the rest of the afternoon until four o'clock count on my bunk. She stood at my gate and talked when the cop let her into the hallway for a shower. She offered to suck my dick but I passed on it. Queen Bee had a reputation for flipping her husband so she ended up on top with his asshole on the bottom. If her partner didn't like it, she was quick to show just how it was she made the Mexican Nationals. I liked to keep my asshole to myself and wasn't looking forward to seeing her boxing career up close, so I kept my distance.

I liked Queen Bee and wished her the best. She

wanted to go to Acapulco and work as a hairdresser
when she got out. In the meantime, she pressed pants
in the laundry and never missed the Monday night
fights, no matter who she was married to.

14

Queen Bee behaved like she did because it made time
pass the way she wanted. The rest of the Mission followed the same rule, myself included.

I found a pattern that worked best and stuck to it.
It was called my routine. Everybody had one.

Weekdays, mine began at six in the morning when
the guard with Birdcage duty turned the light on. The
bulb hanging from my ceiling flashed, and I rolled out
to brush my hair and shave. I always rolled out early to
make sure I'd be ready to leave when the time came.
The Birdcage doors only opened once in the morning
for thirty seconds. If you didn't step out then, you were
locked into your cell when it came time for work call
at 7:30. Missing work meant the Basement, and it was
a common sight to see late wakers finish dressing in the
hall after the door slammed shut again.

Work lasted until 3:30 with a break for lunch and a
half hour to pick up laundry before count at four
o'clock. At 5:30, the Birdcage was released for dinner.
I usually ate quickly and got out to the big exercise

yard early and played as much basketball as I could. At 7:30, whistles were blown from the gun towers and the big yard closed down while we returned to our cells to be counted. When that was done, I went back out to the little yard or hallways until lock-in for the night at 9. I wrote letters until lights out at 10. When I was done, I wanted to sleep and I didn't want to wait half an hour in the dark to do it. That meant I had to be tired, and my routine was designed to get me as much that way as I could manage.

Work was a big help once I found a job I liked.

15

That, however, took a while. My first job just wasn't what I had in mind. When I got out of the Basement, Joe Friday told me to report to Diamond Jim the next morning at the back gate. Diamond Jim was my boss. He told me and forty others to get on the two flatbed trucks, and he followed in his jeep as we drove down the side of the bump to the barn. Diamond Jim had four other cops to help him, but managed to greet me personally. He had Mr. Wingle tell me to come into his office.

When I did, Diamond Jim was sitting behind the desk still wearing his cowboy hat. I looked at him real close on the way in. Diamond Jim appeared to have gotten old and fat at the same time. His cheeks hung like sacks and flopped over the corners of his mouth. Diamond Jim's skin was the color of last week's newspaper. He had my file on his desk.

"Sit down," he said.

I sat on the wooden chair next to the desk.

"In case you don't know it," he continued, "I run this farm. You call me Mr. James. You call him Mr. Wingle." Mr. Wingle was standing behind me in the doorway. As Diamond Jim talked, his eyes bulged and he kept leaning across the desk. "I've been looking at your file," he said, shifting in his seat and pulling his face back. "And I don't want no smart-ass bullshit on my farm. You understand?"

I nodded.

"Work hard and keep your mouth shut and we'll get along. But I'll tell you right now, Mr. Wingle's gonna watch you. If you try to start any riots, I'm gonna have your ass inside in a hot minute."

Diamond Jim leaned back and sucked on his pipe. His face was turning pink.

"I don't start riots," I said.

"Shut up," Diamond Jim answered.

Wingle told me to come on, and I was glad to. He put me to work with six Mexicans in the onion patch. For the next week, the seven of us chopped weeds until it was time to go back inside. Mr. Wingle sat at the edge of the field in his truck and watched. We had a jug of water, and took our breaks squatted around it trying to talk in Pidgin English. When we had our conversation, Wingle usually got out of the cab and leaned on the hood to get a better look.

I did all right my first four days on the job, but the fifth one just seemed to fall apart from the word Go. For starters, I slept so late I had to do my dressing in the hall. When I reported to the back gate, Diamond Jim noticed I hadn't shaved. He didn't say anything at the time, but sent me a message with Mr. Wingle before the day was over.

"Hey, Harris," Wingle called from his truck.

I dropped my hoe and walked over. Wingle smashed a fly against the side of his head. After he'd brushed it off, he looked up.

"Mr. James says to tell ya to shave when we go in for lunch. If ya don't," he continued, "he says he'll shave ya himself."

"How's he gonna do that?" I asked.

"With his pocketknife," Wingle explained.

I swatted at a gnat on my leg, wiped the sweat out of my eyes, and tried to be reasonable with Mr. Wingle.

"Look, Mr. Wingle," I said. "I live in C Block. I can't get into my cell to shave during lunch. The cop spends that hour feeding the Basement."

Wingle shrugged and spit. "I'm just delivering the message," he said. "You talk to him about it."

I got my chance at quitting time. The farm crew was loading into the truck when Wingle told me to come into the office. Inside, Diamond Jim was in back of the desk. As soon as I sat down, he stood up. His cheeks were flapping like chicken wings.

"Don't lie to me," he yelled.

"I haven't said nothin," I answered.

"Shut up."

It wasn't hard to tell Diamond Jim was pissed. He'd turned pink again and his collar was blotted with sweat.

"I know what you're up to," Diamond Jim shouted. A fly buzzed across his desk, and he mashed it with a file. Diamond Jim flicked the insect meat onto the floor and looked straight at me. "Mr. Wingle has told me everything." Diamond Jim paused significantly.

"What am I up to?" I interrupted.

"Will you shut up!" Jim roared.

I shut up.

Diamond Jim walked around to the side of the desk with a rolled-up file in his hand. He tapped the Out basket with it. "You're organizing," he said. "You're tryin to get those Mexicans to go in with you and raise some kinda shit out in my onion patch."

Mr. Wingle reached into his pocket and scratched his ass. "Every day he talks to em," Wingle testified. "All of em all squatted around. I seen em."

"Oh, come on," I whined. "I don't know twenty words of Spanish. You can't be . . ."

Diamond Jim roared again, and shook like one of god's very own farts. "Shut up!" he screamed. "You'll talk when you're asked, you hear?" Diamond Jim had the file cocked over his head.

"I'll talk when I need to," I shouted back.

"Shut up," he screamed again. "Shut up, shut up, shut up."

I shut up. Diamond Jim walked around his filing cabinet. Then he turned and looked at Wingle. "Put him on the trucks," he said. "I'll fix his fucking wagon."

Wingle led me back to the rest of the crew. The heat was rising off the road in waves. The mosquitoes around the ditch were thick as quilts as we drove for the Mission's back gate. I figured I was going to get sent back to the Basement, but that's not the way it happened. Diamond Jim put me to work on the gut truck instead.

Believe me, it was the pits.

16

On the surface, it looked like a promotion. My new job made me a truck driver and I had no qualms about giving up my hoe, but the real drift of the position came across early. The truck I drove carried crews from the back gate to the barn, and milk from the dairy to the kitchen. On Tuesdays and Thursdays, it carried six barrels of pig bowels from the slaughterhouse to a pallet down at the edge of prison property. Diamond Jim showed me how to do it personally. On Tuesday morning, he climbed up to my window. "Stop at the slaughterhouse," he said, "and meet me down by the fence on the back road."

I did what he told me, and came up the back road at twenty miles an hour, carrying six barrels of fresh pig guts. They didn't smell too bad, but when I got to Diamond Jim's truck, I realized they weren't always that way. Twenty yards past the boss, last Thursday's guts were still sitting on the pallet ripe as hell. The dog food company hadn't picked them up like they were supposed to. Each barrel had flies swarming all over it like a coat of hair. The guts inside had swollen in the heat until they ballooned two feet over the barrel's lip to give a sort of ice-cream-cone effect. My stomach jerked, and I had to swallow to keep the bile down. Diamond Jim had a wet handkerchief over his nose.

The boss motioned me out of the cab, and got in behind the wheel. "You just back up to it," he shouted to me, and ground the gearbox into reverse. He inched the rear bumper up to the pallet and into the cans so they fell over with a *splop* and spilled out into the ground. The flies rose like oil smoke and settled in squadrons on the runny five-day-old blood. The wave of smell made me stagger. Diamond Jim pulled the truck up to me and got out. "There's a shovel in the bed," he said, "clean those up and leave the rest."

The job took two hours. I started with my back turned, twenty yards away, and ran in with the shovel and scooped a mound of five-day-old pig into the drum. Then I dropped the shovel and ran back. I did that over and over again, keeping one arm free to fight the flies. When I was done, I stood next to my bumper and puked all over the rear wheels.

I asked Diamond Jim for a new job that night at the back gate. He laughed, and walked away. It was then that I decided to take the situation into my own hands. The way I saw the situation I had one day left to get fired, and planned to give it my best shot.

17

I accomplished my mission before I'd been at work for two hours. My first stop was the tool room, where I borrowed a crescent wrench. After I loaded the kitchen's forty cans of milk at the dairy, I made a few modifications on my '62 Chevy flatbed. First, I unbolted the exhaust manifold, and then I flattened both inside tires on the double back axle. As long as I took the longest way in, I figured that was enough to do the trick.

A network of roads ran around the Mission property. They were all dirt except the main stem leading from the highway to the front door. The shortest route from the dairy to the kitchen was to drive east until I hit the asphalt, then turn left up the slope to the back gate, but I wanted a longer ride. I drove west on the dirt instead. The Chevy sounded fine. Climbing up through the gears, it rumbled like a B-17. I heard the two tires on the back flopping on the other side of the roar. When I reached the fence, I turned north until I hit the road that ran by the graveyard, and turned right. From there it was a straight half-mile to the Mission's back corner, and another right turn to pass under the back tower and arrive at the back gate. I patted the shift knob and popped the clutch. Halfway to the corner, I had the Chevy up to fifty. The milk cans in back were bouncing up and down on the bed with an enormous clanking sound right in back of my head. The engine roared. As I approached the chain-link Mission wall, I went down to third, and the open exhaust popped like a string of land mines. "Wooo-weee," I laughed.

I wanted to get down to second, but I was halfway through the shift when I reached the turn. I muscled the Chevy into the drift and felt my rear end sway as the cans flew into the truck's wooden railing, splatter-ing milk in a wave out the left side and into the dirt. The tires screamed, and I heard the flat one on the left break up into flying pieces of tread. I was fighting the wheel with one arm until I finally got the Chevy straight and into second, just as the front left popped off the rim onto the inside of the axle. The truck's nose dove left and made grinding sounds as it tore up the road. The milk cans rebounded forward and into the back of the cab, knocking the back window into six thousand pieces and onto the seat next to me. The truck stopped in a twenty-foot-high cloud of dust, fifteen yards short of the tower. Mr. Fuck was on duty.

His real name was Buck, but we called him Fuck because he couldn't hear too good when we yelled up at him. He'd taken cover when he first heard the engine firing, and looked up only as I was climbing out of the cab.

"How're things, Mr. Fuck?" I shouted.

"What'd you say?" he answered, leaning his good ear my way.

"Nice day," I said, standing on my running board. Milk was running into the trench the front wheel had dug in the road. The hot engine made popping sounds.

"Shit," Fuck muttered, and got on the phone. Diamond Jim was on the scene of the accident in five minutes. He jumped out of his truck.

"I think my wagon needs fixing," I said with a smile.

I went back to the Basement while my truck went to the shop, but only for a couple of days. After I got out, things turned for the better. I was put to work with the stack crew, and liked it fine. We were a team of convicts who'd fucked up at their other jobs and were reduced to pure labor. The stack crew was sent wherever there was something in the institution that needed to be made into a pile. We stacked everything from hay bales to old bunk beds, and I loved it. I worked hard and soaked my T-shirts with sweat. The exercise left me good and tired at four o'clock. Which is the reason I went to work in the first place.

18

For me, 4 to 5:30 was the hardest hour and a half of the day. I sat on the bottom shelf of the double bunk and leaned my head on the back wall. The afternoon light was confined to a square, lapping over the edge of the shitter. I took my boots off, and waited for the cop to bring the mail.

As much as I loved to get it, mail call was a guaranteed bummer, one way or the other. If I didn't get any letters, I felt abandoned and trapped. I wondered if anything I'd left behind was still there. I paced a lot and figured I didn't really belong anyplace but the place I was. I wanted desperately to know I mattered outside the Mission's walls, but on the days no mail came, I didn't have any proof.

The days letters did arrive weren't any easier. In the whole time I was locked up, I never received one that wasn't opened first. The Mission had a hack working a full shift, just slitting them open and reading. Most of those I got were from Joanie, and it bothered me to have some gray-suited son of a bitch reading what she had to tell me. Sometimes it was good and sometimes it was bad, but all the time it passed under his eyes first. That must have been one of the things that made me read them as hard as I did. I always tried to find more than what was there. I read the lines over and over, trying to figure out what they really meant. Doing that tangled me up in everything I'd left. It made me think of places and people I couldn't get next to, and made me want to know about them. Which is a dead end. Sooner or later in the process, I always ended up admitting it didn't matter. It was no use to wonder, because I couldn't do anything about it anyway.

Admitting that too often takes a lot of steam out of anybody, and I was no exception. I felt bad as a motherfucker whenever a mail call came up. I got used to it after a while, but I never did learn not to care. I just took my pain as it came, and walked it off whenever I got the chance.

19

Walking was an anesthetic we all used. It's an old folk medicine cure for time. In the evening, convicts were walking all over the Mission. Both little yards and all the hallways were walked. The dormitory aisles, the weight pile, and the big yard were all walked, too. The big yard most of all. That's where the heaviest walking took place. Out there, you could set a good pace and go yards without turning around and starting back the way you came.

Walking partners were one of the essentials of Mission life. We all walked in packs. I usually matched strides with Pablo, Guano, J.C., Old Robert, or the Carrot, when I wasn't on the basketball court. Sometimes we talked and sometimes we didn't, but we always passed the weight pile, the handball courts, and the furniture factory; walked under the gaze of the back tower, and we were on the big yard. The fence was topped with three rolls of concertina wire strung up from post to post like a disease. Three gun towers watched over it all. Mr. Fuck manned the first one, Officer Bruno the second, and the Okie sat in the third, on the east side. If it wasn't for the Okie, I'd probably have left prison without a good feeling about anything I saw there with a badge. I learned to like the Okie one night in July when the Carrot and I took two laps along the fence in an attempt to wear off the last traces of his meeting with Gyro Gearloose.

During the time I spent in the Mission, the Carrot and I got close. This sentence was his third time down the line. The first was for burglary in the state of New Mexico. Then he lost an armed robbery case to California. When California popped him, he was out on bail from a charge the feds had waiting in Albuquerque. The feds wanted him for possession of heroin, but Carrot wasn't worried about their charges at first. He'd already begun doing his state time at San Quentin when the feds transported him east for trial. Carrot left Quentin optimistic. He told his cellie that he'd be back soon with no more time. "Illegal search" is what his lawyer called it. The lawyer set out to prove his point with the government's first witness, a narc named Charlie Brown.

"Why, Officer Brown," Carrot's lawyer asked, "did you stop the defendant's car on the night in question?"

The narc answered in a textbook tone of voice. "We had good information," he explained, "that Mr. Carrot was in possession of a large quantity of heroin."

"What do you mean when you say good information?"

"It is information from a reliable source, a source we used before, and had always proved reliable."

Carrot's lawyer wound up and delivered what he expected to be the blow that knocked the case off the docket. "Can the government actually produce this supposed source?" he asked with an edge on his voice. "Is that source present to be identified?"

"We certainly can," the narc grinned. "She's there in the second row. Mrs. Alvin Carrot." Carrot turned and looked back over the short fence in front of the gallery, and saw his wife stand up. He changed his plea to guilty, and went back with five years to do for the Attorney General whenever California finished with him. He went straight to the Mission a year later with a stop at the Tucson jail on the way.

The Carrot had just been to see Gyro Gearloose that morning. Gyro Gearloose was the supervisor of the Mission's education department. He controlled the night school and had to approve all books and magazine subscriptions. When Carrot submitted a request to receive the *Evergreen Review*, Gearloose called him in.

"It's about this subscription request," Gyro said. He adjusted his glasses on his slide-rule nose, and looked at the slip. "It's for a magazine called *Evergreen Review*, is that right?"

"That's right," the Carrot said.

"What do you know about this magazine?"

"I just saw it advertised in another magazine, and it looked good," Carrot lied. He'd once seen a copy Chester had, and read a story in it about a woman who fucked her TV.

"It's filth," Gearloose interrupted. His teeth were set, and ground on each other. "The captain gave me these copies he found in a shakedown." Gyro held up the very magazine Carrot had read. "They're shocking," the education director went on. "This one has an article about masturbation." Gearloose swallowed, and his Adam's apple bounced.

"No shit?" Carrot said. He reached across the desk and started leafing through the issue.

"Put that down," Gearloose admonished. "This is serious."

Gyro Gearloose took the copies he'd displayed and deposited them in the desk drawer. Then he turned back to Carrot. "Tell me, Carrot," he said, "do you have a sister?"

"Yah," Carrot answered, "I've got one sixteen years old."

"Would you want her to read this kind of trash?"

Carrot rubbed his jaw for a minute and then leaned forward in his chair. "You know what, Mr. Gearloose? I've been locked up for a year and a half on this one, and I was a long time in Quentin before that. You know what, Mr. Gearloose?" Carrot finished, "I'd like to fuck my sister."

The Carrot never got his *Evergreen Review*. Gyro Gearloose terminated their conversation and sent Carrot back to his job in the warehouse. He walked off his disappointment that night in the big yard with me and El Presidente.

The sky was bleeding as the sun retreated onto the other side of the tower. In the middle of our second lap, the Okie gave us all proof of his good intentions.

20

It happened all of a sudden. There were about seventy-five men out in the yard at the time. One of them was a kid who'd only arrived two days earlier from San Antonio. When our walking party turned behind the softball backstop, he went for the blind corner with traveling on his mind.

The big yard had four corners and only three towers. The kid went for the empty space, thinking to slip over and run for cover in the badlands. He made it up the fence with no problems, but the wire on top grabbed him like a swarm of bees. Mr. Fuck saw the body on its way over and hit the alarm. The kid was stuck there, wiggling and struggling to unhook from the barbs, and drop over to the other side. Twenty-seven different horns sounded, and every gray suit in the Mission came running.

Frosty and the Snake Charmer, two lieutenants, led the charge. They ran out for the yard, strapping .38s around their waists. The Snake Charmer fell down once on the way to the back gate. He had a walkie-talkie with him, and shouted orders to the towers. "Kill the son of a bitch," the Snake Charmer said.

Mr. Fuck ripped off a clip, but he couldn't hit the kid. He had to shoot catty-corner across the yard, and shooting down from a height is the hardest shot there is. Bruno tried too, but did no better. The kid was still wiggling, with zings all around him, and almost made it over when the Okie leaned out the window. He was a dead shot, and had the shortest one to make. The Snake Charmer was screaming into the radio, and the sirens shook the roof. The Okie switched his radio off, pointed his rifle straight up in the sky, and emptied his clip at a pair of clouds wandering over the desert. The kid dropped down outside, and the two lieutenants ran him down in a patrol jeep twenty yards into the sagebrush. He came back inside in chains, and went straight to the Basement.

I saw the Okie in the front hallway the next day.

"How come," I asked, "you didn't kill that dude last night? You had him set up."

The Okie didn't smile. "I got no business killin anybody," he said.

The Okie'd never passed the tenth grade, and got his last promotion eight years earlier. He got a check every week, needed four more years to make his pension, and had enough sense to know the difference between murder and work.

He was an exception.

21

Joe Friday was a lot closer to the real model than the Okie. He was what we called a promotion hack, a man looking to make his way up by stepping on as many folks as he could. Joe Friday was only two steps short of lieutenant, and rising fast. When he got through with the Cleaner, he was even closer than that.

The Cleaner lived in Number 1 right by the door, and kept the cell block mopped and swept. He was slow, but decent. It was his job to issue fresh sheets on Thursdays, and keep the box of free tobacco and papers stocked. The Cleaner spent most of the day in his cell by himself. He'd been put in the Birdcage because of his nerves, which made him hard to get along with in a group living situation. He'd been in a dormitory until the noise set him off in a rage that took three police to stop. When I knew him, the Cleaner picked up a dose of tranquilizers three times a day at the hospital, and stayed out of most everybody's way. His only real mistake was walking into Joe Friday's sights. Friday was looking to better himself, and the Cleaner just happened to be handy.

Joe Friday was a success because he understood how promotions worked. Guards got raises by gaining the praise of their superiors, and nothing pleased the captain like enforcing the rules. Even if you had to invent a little to fill in the rough edges. At the first Monday staff meeting in July, John Wayne warned everybody to be on the lookout for weapons. His snitches told him shit was in the air, and he wanted the place cleaned up. Joe Friday got the message loud and clear.

When he came back to the block, Friday sent the Cleaner over to the warehouse for more toilet paper. Then he opened the Cleaner's cell and hid a homemade shank in the mattress. It was just six inches or so of roughed-out steel, but in the Mission that counted as a knife. Two hours later, John Wayne came through on a shakedown and was looking over Friday's shoulder when the weapon was discovered. Joe Friday spread-eagled the Cleaner in the hall and frisked his pockets.

"All right, buddy," he growled, "talk fast and talk straight. Where'd you get the knife?"

"I ain't never seen that thing," the Cleaner pleaded. "That shank ain't mine. Honest it ain't."

"Tell it to the captain," Friday answered.

"I swear, Captain . . ."

John Wayne looked over to Friday. "Take him downstairs," he said.

The Cleaner got back from the Basement in time for August. Joe Friday got promoted to safety officer, and wasn't on the block when the Cleaner came back. A hack we called the Evil Stepmother took Friday's place. Friday's last act had been to cut the Cleaner's pill dose down, and the Cleaner showed it. He paced his cell a lot and asked for more. Late at night, after lights out, I could hear him kicking his gate and pleading. "Officer," he said, "I got to get more medicine. Man, I can't sleep. I can't relax cause I'm so nervous."

None of his pleas worked, but the Cleaner seemed to get over the hump without help. By August 6, he seemed to have calmed down, and started the day in the front of breakfast line. The Cleaner worked all day scrubbing out the empty cells and polishing the hallway. When I got in from work, the Birdcage was spotless, and the Cleaner was ahead of schedule. Usually the cop let him out of his cell after count to finish his sweep, but on the sixth of August he stayed on his bunk. The Cleaner had a plan. If events had followed their usual pattern, it would have worked. Usually, the hack counted us first and then went down to the Basement to get a total there. Then he walked back to the Control Room to report. All in all, the guard was often off the block for fifteen minutes, plenty of time for what the Cleaner had in mind.

As soon as the Evil Stepmother headed downstairs, the Cleaner took a fresh razor blade and slashed his throat from ear to ear. His blood splashed on the blankets, and he lay back on the mattresses to watch his life drip away. The Cleaner figured he had plenty of time to die without interruption. He missed his calculation, but not by much. It was only an accident that he lived. The Evil Stepmother walked off without his pen, and came back to find the Cleaner leaking into the hall.

The Cleaner's blood was spreading across the floor like maple syrup. The Evil Stepmother yanked the cell open and carried the Cleaner over his shoulder to the hospital. The nurse stitched his jugular vein, and saved the Cleaner's life. When he was done, the nurse said another minute and the big Mexican would have had it. That evening, the Stepmother was late with the mail delivery, and we didn't get out for dinner until six o'clock.

The sun was still shining its last light when my cell finally opened. The six o'clock shine fell on the hall from a single high window on the wall at the end of the block. It cast shadows that ran in gutters up to the Cleaner's house and through the gate. We got out for dinner one cell at a time, and I was last. When I walked past Number 1, the floor was still covered with the Cleaner's juice. It had spread across the hall to the lip of the shower. To get dinner, the Birdcage had to walk through the puddle. When I got to the head of the hall, the blood was tracked past the second door and out of the block. It was the color of plums and had begun to crust around the edges. The blood was splashed all over the Cleaner's cell. He'd left one hand-print on the wall, like he was signing a painting or maybe cashing a check.

22

The job Joe Friday did on the Cleaner was a little heavier than most. The standard brand wasn't so obvious, and lasted a lot longer. In my first six months at the Mission, I got a good taste of it. I learned hacks are paid to keep convicts off step, to keep them from ever being sure, to summon their pain and tie them up with it. The Attorney General calls it "controlling the population." What that meant in real life was fucking with folks in a lot of little ways, just to make sure they didn't take anything for granted. Too much muscle in the process was unproductive. Behind the walls, the law worked best when it swarmed like gnats.

Because of my reputation, I got a lot of that technique. Long after Warden Gruff went on to a new assignment, I was still labeled a "troublemaker," and got a lot of attention for it. I got questioned regularly and given a lot of on-the-spot education about regulations. In August, I got my hair cut in the typical style.

The ritual took place at five in the morning. I was stretched out on my bunk, asleep in the dark, when Bilbo, the man on night shift, came up to my door with his flashlight. He shone it in my face. I felt the light on my eyes like something very far away. I dreamed someone was frying my face like an egg, and woke up with a blink.

"What the fuck?"

"Roll out," Bilbo said.

"What?"

"Roll out."

I swung my legs to the floor and scratched myself. My first thought was transfer. They're moving me on to Leavenworth, I figured.

"Where am I going?" I asked.

"You don't got to know that," Bilbo answered. "Just get dressed."

I did, and he walked me down the dark block, opened the door, and led me out into the hallway. It was completely empty. Our steps ran ahead of us in echoes along the floor. When we got down to the main corridor, I saw light leaking under the barbershop door. We headed straight for it, and walked inside.

I blinked in the bright light. So did Sandoval, the barber. He was so sure he was going to Leavenworth when the cops woke him up, that he gave his watch to Bad News, his buddy from El Paso. Sandoval was standing by the chair, yawning with his clippers in his hand. Three other members of the night shift were sitting on the waiting bench along the wall. They laughed when I came in. So did Bilbo. He walked over to the poster on the wall and pointed to a marine crew-cut photograph.

"Give him one of those," Bilbo laughed.

Sandoval spared as much of my hair as he could, but I felt the wind on the sides of my head when I finally left. The Mission was awake by then, and I caught an early breakfast. Afterward, I went out in the little yard and waited for work call. The sky still seemed groggy and hadn't reached the chill in the corners. The Evil Stepmother, with his lunch bucket, passed me on his way into work.

"How are you this morning?" I asked.

"Tuck your shirt in," he answered.

23

In the face of the Attorney General's attitude, I learned to front off. I learned to hide my weaknesses behind my face and never let on what I really felt. I did so as a matter of course. If I didn't, the law could locate my pain and I knew from experience it would do everything it could to walk all over that spot. I learned that much every time I had a visit. Out with my other life, the cops knew I was vulnerable and made the most of it.

Especially Jungle Jim. Come September, he took it upon himself to make my visits as miserable as possible.

On weekends, Jungle Jim worked the visiting yard with Greaseball. It was easy to see why the Attorney General had stationed them there. They looked on it as their responsibility to make the place as much like the rest of the prison as they could.

They had a good start on it before they even began.

The visiting area looked like everything else at the Mission except for the plastic plants, couches, and vending machines. The plants were four feet tall, and distributed around the room's corners. The biggest one was near the table Greaseball sat at by the door leading out to the yard. On sunny days, we sat out there on benches and folding chairs.

It was a sunny September day when I got my first visit under the gaze of Jungle Jim and Greaseball. Each prisoner is allowed a maximum of ten hours a month out there, either on Friday, Saturday, or Sunday. Joanie and I usually spread ours out over the whole weekend and called it a month.

I knew I had a visit on Friday when the speakers broadcast my name. "Harris, 4697," they crackled, "visit."

That was the cue for the Evil Stepmother to open my cell door. Then he opened the gate and the outside door. All that took five minutes, and got me as far as the upstairs hall. When I got down the steps, I reported to the Control Room, "Harris, 4697," I said to the cop behind the bulletproof glass. "Visit."

He looked at his clipboard. "Harris," he said, "4697, visit," checked my name off, and buzzed the electric lock on the gate. I walked down the front hallway to the shakedown room. Jungle Jim ran the operation there.

Going into a visit, each of us was frisked. Coming out, we had to strip and stand inspection at all orifices. As soon as I walked in, Jungle Jim told me to put my hands over my head and slapped the sides of my legs. When he was done, I walked toward the last gate and waited for him to buzz it open. Standing behind the bars, I could see Joanie and the kid. They waved, I felt my insides rush toward them, and Jungle Jim grabbed me by the shirt.

"What's this?" he asked, pointing at my sideburns.

"My sideburns," I answered. "Why don't you open the gate?"

"Come on, Harris," Jungle Jim answered back, "I can't let you go out there lookin like that. Those sideburns are at least a half inch too long. What are all those folks from the outside world gonna think? We got to show em a little grooming. You're gonna have to go back and trim em before you visit."

"What're you talking about?" I argued. Deep inside I wanted to split his skull in half with the fire extinguisher hanging off the wall. "My sideburns have been this way for a month and nobody said nothin."

"I said it now," Jungle Jim growled. "If you want to visit, you better get back and get regulation."

I walked back to the electric lock, got buzzed through, and climbed the stairs to the Birdcage door. After pounding on it for a minute or two, the Stepmother came up from the Basement and let me in. I shaved a quarter inch off the bottom of my sideburns, then yelled for him to open me up. He did, and I returned the same way I'd come. Jungle Jim told me I looked real handsome when I came through shakedown the second time. Then he opened the gate and let me visit.

It was hot that afternoon, so we sat on the lawn. Joanie took the baby's clothes off and let him play in the drip from the faucet on the visiting yard wall. It was another world out there, and I didn't get in any more trouble until Friday's visiting was done.

Then I got my next dose. After Jungle Jim had finished inspecting my asshole and having me lift my nutsack so he could check the underside for contraband, he told me to see the lieutenant. Right then I knew I had more shit in store. It was Frosty's shift in the lieutenant's office, and he worked hand in glove with Jungle Jim. Jungle Jim closed the door in back of us, so we were in the office alone.

"Look, Harris," Frosty said, "my window here looks out on the yard, and I've been watching you today. I don't like getting on your case, but I've been getting complaints."

"From who?"

"The ladies in the records office, among others," he said. The records office window overlooked the visiting yard.

"What'd I do?"

Frosty shifted in his chair and looked off at the wall. "You got to get some clothes on that kid of yours," he said. "There's women and children out there, and that boy of yours is half naked all the time."

"But he's only ten months old."

"Tough shit," Frosty finished. "You keep pants on him anyway." The lieutenant motioned for me to leave. I left the door open on my way out, and headed for the Birdcage. I had another visit to look forward to all night long. After dark, I tried to picture my son with my eyes closed and my heart wide open. It never quite came into focus so I gave up and went to sleep.

24

Saturday was a little different. On the second day of our visit, Greaseball carried the action. He started by taking the handle off the faucet so it couldn't drip anymore. Then he waited and watched with his eyes popped on the top of his head like a toad. It didn't take him long to see something he didn't like.

Joanie and I were in the habit of sitting together in the far corner of the yard where it was hard for the Greaseball to watch. We spread a blanket in the shade and tried to talk.

"What do you think the Parole Board's going to do this time?" she asked.

"I don't know," I said. "I go up again next month and everybody says I'll get a date. But there's no way to tell. If they don't give me one, I've just got another year to do without their help."

"Do you think they'll let you out?"

"I don't know," I repeated. I swatted at one of the flies swarming around our sandwiches. "I don't know."

We were quiet for a while and then she spoke up again. "It's going to be hard," she said.

"It ain't easy now."

"I know," she said, "you've changed."

I looked off at the fence and the tower beyond that. "It's true," I admitted.

When I looked back at her, Joanie had started to cry. Just a soft cry that started in her lip and spread up to her eyes. I put her head on my shoulder and looked for someplace to cry myself.

That's when Greaseball jumped in. He came running across the yard blowing his whistle. "Stop that," he screamed. "I can see you. Stop that right now."

In five minutes, I was back in Frosty's office for the second day in a row. Frosty and Jungle Jim were both there.

"Florez caught him trying to put his hands in his wife's pants," Jungle Jim explained.

I jumped out of my chair and let it all loose. "You're a lying cocksucker," I yelled. "She was crying on my shoulder."

Frosty told me to shut up and wait outside the office in the hall. After ten minutes, he called me back in. Jungle Jim left as I sat down.

"I warned you about behaving," Frosty opened. "It's disgusting. If you can't act any better than that, you're not going to get a chance to do it again."

To keep me in line, the lieutenant assigned me to Jungle Jim full time. When I came out for Sunday's visit, I was told I'd have to visit in a room all by myself with Jungle Jim sitting between me and my wife. I wouldn't do it, and she wouldn't, either.

"Fuck a bunch of visits," I said.

Jungle Jim let us kiss good-by, and I went back to the Birdcage and stayed locked up the rest of the day. She said she'd see me next month, and headed for California. I didn't think about it and spent the afternoon trying to forget.

25

After a while in the Mission, I got good at it. Forgetting became one of my major skills. Thanks to the Attorney General, I learned to turn my memory on and off at will. I could lie on my back and think about the streets until it got me off, then throw a switch in my head and come back to where I lived without looking back once. I thought about my other life just enough to get a good tingle and a mellow stroke, but never enough to get down. Never enough to miss it, never enough to make me admit I wasn't there, never enough to lose control. I credit a lot of my survival to the technique. Without it, I would have always been at the mercy of places I wasn't.

As strong as I got at it, visits were always another kind of question. I never cut the visits off in my head. I savored them and watched them slowly fade. I plucked pieces out for future use, and swept out the leavings when they lost their glow. Sometimes they held on and wouldn't let go. Then most of my attempts were fruitless. The run-in with Jungle Jim in September was one of those.

I lay on my bunk all afternoon. Things on the block had changed some. The Mission was overcrowded and everybody in Maximum Security got doubled up. Except the birds. They weren't allowed roommates. The Stepmother moved my old friend Curly from the Basement and gave him the mattress over my head. He'd been out visiting on Saturday and knew how I felt. He knew nobody gets over a visit right away. I stared at the glare in the hallway for a long time. I had the Parole Board on my mind.

After an hour, Curly hung his head over the edge. "What's up, Ace?" he said.

I cocked my head back. "It sure wouldn't bother me a bit if those motherfuckers cut me loose next month," I confessed. "I could stand a vacation."

Curly said he could see my point, and went back to his yoga. I imagined how the door would sound when it opened the very last time. The noise would be clear as a bell, and dying fast.

26

As my meeting with the Parole Board approached, I thought about it a lot. I started getting superstitious and watched for all the signs of future luck. I counted omens. The biggest omen of all appeared two nights before the parole judge arrived. The Fairy Godmother told me about it over dinner on the second Monday in October.

The Fairy Godmother was just an old sissy now, but she'd had glory in her day. Curly and I usually shared a chow hall table with her, and got on good terms. In Kansas, she'd been known as the Petticoat Bandit, and did six banks before the law caught on. She robbed in drag and her outfit kept the police off her scent for a long time. Dressed like a hundred-dollar whore with a .38 in each hand, she terrorized vaults from Kansas City to Topeka until the police surrounded her hideout in St. Louis. The Fairy Godmother came out the front door in a beige suit and pillbox hat with veil. She blew the leg off a member of the Kansas State Police and took six slugs herself. The cops never figured out what she really was until they handcuffed her to the turnkey. Her skirt was all ripped up and the sergeant took a peek. "Jesus Christ," he said, "this broad's got a dick." After that, they felt free to kick her and did, all the way to the emergency room.

Kansas kept the Fairy Godmother for twenty years. Afterward, she was out long enough to hijack a truck and pick up five to do for the feds. She worked the night shift at the hospital, and had been on duty Sunday evening when the Valentine Factory died.

The Valentine Factory was one of the hospital's steady residents. He was an old man, and had been living in one of the wards for the last year and a half. Sometimes his lungs filled up and sometimes his arthritis ached, but mostly he just made valentines and watched TV. The Valentine Factory was trying to finish twenty-five years, and was six months short when he left the hard way. He made Christmas and Easter cards too, but valentines were his specialty. He made them with construction paper, sequins, and bits of ribbon. A good one cost four packs. I paid him six for a custom-made card to send to Joanie on our anniversary.

"To my wife of these years," he wrote in sequins, "may our love prosper and reach over these bleak walls." I thought it was a little stiff, but he considered it one of the best he'd ever done.

When business was slow, the Valentine Factory stuck to the TV. His favorite program was "Let's Make A Deal." He liked to watch the endless succession of appliances and outboard motors. More than that, he liked to root.

"Take that washing machine," he'd yell across the ward at the box on the wall, "and stick it in your ear. Better yet, stick it in that faggot announcer's scabby asshole." When the Valentine Factory finished an outburst, he'd turn to whoever else was in the room, and chuckle. He loved the excitement and it helped his circulation.

The Valentine Factory started out in Minneapolis with his pet dog. It was some kind of collie mongrel. The animal was just about all he owned except for a couple of the best ten-dollar printing plates the Secret Service had ever seen. When the cops pulled up in front of the Valentine Factory's hotel, he took his dog, made it down the fire escape, and headed south as quick as he could go. When the Valentine Factory got to New Mexico, he printed the perfect University of New Mexico Music Department pension check. He printed forty-seven of them to be exact. Number 36 bounced before he got to the bank door, and since then the Valentine Factory had been making his way back to Minneapolis one day at a time. God and the doctor willing, he'd have been there in another six months.

God never said how He felt, but Coat Rack, the doctor, nixed the deal before He got a chance. Coat Rack was skinny, and seemed to have very little idea of what he was doing. He'd gone through medical school working nights, and the amount of knowledge and skill he picked up seemed to be minimal as a result. Coat Rack wasn't mean like Jekyll, he was just incompetent and frightened by the fact. Those who liked him said he knew that he didn't know how to be a doctor, he was just scared to admit it. A confession like that could ruin his career. So Coat Rack carried on, and offed the Valentine Factory in the process.

It all began on Saturday when the Valentine Factory reported chest pains and trouble breathing. The Fairy Godmother told the cop on duty, and Coat Rack came in on his day off to make a diagnosis. He figured heart attack, and had the Valentine Factory treated accordingly. The Godmother had her doubts, saying it looked more like pneumonia to her, but Coat Rack wouldn't hear her. Sunday, the Valentine Factory was showing signs of dying. The hospital called Dr. Rack again, and Coat Rack came back for another look. The Fairy Godmother said they ought to send him to El Paso, where he could get full treatment.

Coat Rack looked down at the Valentine Factory. He was tossing in the bed, sucking air, and mumbling. "I can't do that," Coat Rack said. "What would the doctors down there think of me if I sent a man down there in this condition. We'll wait until he comes up a bit."

On Sunday around 2 A.M., the Valentine Factory's kidneys failed and he died. The Fairy Godmother held his hand on his way out of the world. The Bureau of Prisons shipped his body to his daughter in St. Paul.

"I tell ya, honey," the Fairy Godmother complained over Monday's chili and rice, "that doctor up there don't know his head from his tail. He should be shot for what he done to that poor man. If he tried to doctor me, I'd tell him to kiss my cunt." She talked with her mouth full. "That's just what I'd tell him."

I slid my tray into the dish room on the way out of the chow hall. Out in the corridor, I stopped at the bulletin board and read the Transfer Sheet posted there. The Transfer Sheet was a mimeographed list, posted daily to record changes in any inmate's status. It was divided into three columns: one for names and numbers, one marked "From," and one marked "To." I found the Valentine Factory's name halfway down the sheet. "From" was "Hospital," and "To" was "Deceased."

Next to the Transfer Sheet was a second mimeograph for Tuesday's parole hearings. I was listed beside 10:30. I stared at my name and number for a while, and then headed for the big yard to get a little exercise before it closed to give the cops a chance to count.

27

At 10:30, the clerk called my name, and I left my seat in the corridor to walk through the varnished door and see the Parole Board. The hearing room was paneled in wood of dark shades. The board was a bald man with eyes like dinner plates, and his sixty-six-year-old secretary. Flanked by the American flag and Errol Flynn, they made a nice couple.

The bald man asked me if I would be willing to soldier if I was sent to Israel instead of Indochina. I told him I'd think about it, but offhand I had to say I wasn't all that interested in working for the government, wherever they had in mind to send me. The secretary recorded our conversation in shorthand. Errol Flynn jumped in every now and then to kiss the bald man's ass if he looked like he needed it.

"Harris has been one of our problem cases," he explained, "but at heart, I think he's a good risk."

The bald man nodded his head a lot, and finally said it was time for me to leave. As usual, I was told I'd hear from the board in a while. This time I knew what a while meant, and I didn't have to be told anything more. I'd become pretty good at waiting since the last time we'd met. I'd learned there wasn't any other choice.

If I didn't want to wait and I didn't want to leave the way the Valentine Factory did, I'd have had to run off. I never did consider running as a serious option, and I only felt more so as time passed. Living so close to Fast Feet reinforced my feeling.

28

Some said escape was a hobby, some said it was a disease, but Fast Feet always said he did it because he needed to. Fast Feet lived in Number 9, just close enough to me that I could see half of his cell through my gate. He learned about escape the hard way.

Fast Feet started his time with a sentence of four years for stealing a car. He was sent to a federal kid joint in Oklahoma on his nineteenth birthday. Six months later, he got a letter from Mom saying Dad was in the hospital and likely to die. Fast Feet took his letter to the warden with a request.

"Warden," he said, "my daddy's dyin in San Antone. Can't you let me go see him? You can send two cops with me, just let me see him before he's gone."

The warden said Fast Feet hadn't done enough of his time to get any such privilege.

"But he's dyin," Fast Feet pleaded.

"Tough," said the warden. "You shoulda thought about that before you lifted that Buick."

That night, Fast Feet went over the wall. The FBI staked out his father's hospital room, and the judge gave Fast Feet five more years. Fast Feet went back to Oklahoma and got two of them done before he got a letter from his uncle saying his mother'd been killed in a car wreck. The funeral was in two days. Like all letters, the cops read it before anybody else, and locked Fast Feet up before they delivered it. When the funeral was over, the warden let Fast Feet out of lockup. Fast Feet hit the fence again that night. The FBI found him in the graveyard, and the judge gave Fast Feet five more to stack on top of what he already had. Just for insurance, they transferred him to Leavenworth to do it.

Fast Feet let his bets ride awhile at Leavenworth, and filed a writ for rehearing in court. After a year, the marshals drove him to Duke City to see the judge. Before he got there, Fast Feet tried to jump a turnkey in the county jail. He got as far as the last door, and found he didn't have a key to open it. When he finally got to court, it was just a short stop to pick up another nickel.

Fast Feet had to do that five and one more before he could get another appeal heard, but he took advantage of the opportunity when it came. This time, he stole a handcuff key and jumped the marshals on the highway. He chained them around a tree off to one side of the road and drove their car to Tucson. He ditched it there, and thumbed west. When he got to L.A., Fast Feet found work as a machinist named Billy McCormick. McCormick saved his money, and married a secretary at the plant. He got a loan from the finance company and bought a house. Everything smelled of roses until he stopped getting along with his wife. She threw a vase at him and called the FBI with news of an escaped prisoner working down at the tool factory. This time the judge looked at Fast Feet with a touch of admiration.

"You proved you could make it on the streets," he lectured, "so I won't give you any more time. You just go back and do what you've got left."

Fast Feet thanked the judge and went back to Leavenworth. By the time he got to the Mission, he had less than a year left. He'd lost most of his teeth, but he had good dentures and a sense of hope.

It was his sense of hope that led Fast Feet into the arms of Mickey Rooney and his cousin. Mickey Rooney and Fast Feet lived right across the hall from each other.

29

Mickey Rooney was from a village south of the border, outside of Zacatecas. He got letters from his sister and cousin every week. They were all in Spanish, which is just about all they and Mickey Rooney spoke. Fast Feet was pretty good at English, but that was it. Even so, true love conquered all. Or something like that. I monitored the rise of their romance through October and November. It all started the week after I went to the Parole Board when Fast Feet shouted across the hall after mail call. He was talking to Mickey Rooney.

"Who you gettin all them letters from?" Fast Feet asked.

Mickey Rooney looked up.

"Who-you-get-letters-from?" he repeated, pointing at the envelopes.

"From sister and cousin," Mickey Rooney finally answered.

"Nice?" Fast Feet questioned.

"*Mucho. Grand melones,*" Mickey Rooney said, and slapped his chest.

"Which one?"

Rooney looked blank, so Fast Feet tried again.

"*Qui? Melones,*" he said, "*qui melones?*" and slapped his T-shirt.

Mickey Rooney snapped. "Cousin," he said, slapping his chest again.

"Write her," Fast Feet said, "and ask if I can write her, too."

Rooney got Joe in Number 10 to translate, and then shook his head yes.

"Tell him I'm on the up-and-up," Fast Feet added in Joe's direction. "Say I'm an honorable man, and I got no intentions of violating any of his customs. Tell him to ask her father's permission if he wants to."

Mickey Rooney agreed to it all, and Fast Feet spent a week composing his first letter. He read it to Joe for translation. I listened while bending over my sink to wash.

"Dear Señorita," Fast Feet wrote, "I am writing you because I know your cousin. He says you are a good woman and a virgin. I am in prison now, but I'm not a criminal. I made a mistake, but I have paid for it dearly. I am looking for a woman who will cook and sew and not run around with anybody else. I will work hard for her and give her a good home in Los Angeles where I plan to work, making machines. I am an honest man and I have never beat a woman ever. Yours truly, Bill McCormick."

"No," Fast Feet added, "change that to Richard Walker. I'm gonna start fresh this time."

Mickey Rooney's cousin had to ride twenty miles on a mule to get the letter, and another twenty miles to send an answer, but she answered in two weeks.

"Señor," she wrote, "my cousin is right in the telling you I am well behaved. My father has raised me strict. I am only seventeen, but as you can see, I write and read. I would never marry a man who beat me, and when I marry I will love my husband and my family. I would like to see the United States. I have never been there, but I hear it is beautiful and everybody lives well. I have six sisters and four brothers, and my father is a farmer. He says some Americans are nice people and that you sound like one. I hope you will write back."

Fast Feet did. There was a total of six letters exchanged in the next two months. By November, Fast Feet had a Spanish dictionary, and wouldn't let anybody read the letters. He was a little worried because she hadn't sent the picture she'd promised, but Mickey Rooney must have described her a hundred and twenty times. Fast Feet always got a little confused at the part where he had to convert kilograms into pounds, but he seemed satisfied.

"When I get out," he bragged through the gap in his jaw, "I'm goin south and ask her daddy for her hand. Yes I am." Fast Feet planned to raise the cash for a honeymoon with the American Express game. He would use his savings to buy a load of traveler's checks. Then he would report them lost, and cash both the new and old ones before the computer had a chance to catch up. "Double your money every time," he claimed.

When I finally left the Mission, Fast Feet was supposed to get out three days later. He said he was going to Niagara Falls to get married, and was planning to stop and see me on his way back to L.A., but he never did.

30

I waited through October, November, and most of December for word from the Parole Board. In the meantime, I said good-by a lot. The wind sweeping across the yard got steady, cold, and full of sand. One by one, the people I was closest to went up on the Transfer Sheet marked "Released." Jewell left at the end of October, J.C. right before Christmas, and Pablo got a date in January. Each one of them got short before he left.

Getting short is all part of the Attorney General's game. As the day the front door would open approached, those about to be freed exist in a limbo. They weren't here and they weren't there. Short-timers begin to fade, to lose focus on all those they are about to leave behind. For those of us who had to stay, it was a matter of self-defense. No one took a short man seriously. If they did, he would be missed when he left, and missing people is a prisoner's suicide. We kidded the short-timers, but didn't have much else to say. Inside my head, I retrieved the parts of myself I'd left in my friends' care, to keep from being crippled when they left. I cut them loose and tied my ropes elsewhere. I said I'd see them on the streets, but that was mostly talk. I didn't even know the streets really existed. I was still long, quite a distance in every way from short. The only concrete I saw ahead of me was shaped into walls.

But that all changed overnight. I went to bed the night of December 22, deep in the tunnel, and woke up short on the twenty-third. I found out about it at nine in the morning. Errol Flynn had me brought to his office.

"Sit down," he said.

I sat down.

"The Parole Board," he read from the slip in front of him, "has approved your release on the fifteenth of March."

I experienced a sudden flash behind my eyes. When I looked down at my khakis and out the window at the tower, it all seemed temporary. I felt sweat collecting on my chest.

"That, of course," Flynn added, "is conditional on your behavior between now and March. But I expect you'll have no problems."

I left Errol Flynn's office smiling. I seemed to float over the linoleum and past the chow hall. I buttoned my jacket and stepped out into the little yard leading to the back gate. The wind had stopped and the day felt crisp around my ears. I found Pablo on the bench by the handball court. He saw me coming toward him.

"How'd you do?" he shouted.

"Yeeeeeeeeeeehah," I yelled.

"All right," Pablo grinned, "all fuckin right."

I sat down next to him with the intention of talking about it, but there wasn't much of anything left to say. Instead, we watched the sun creep over until it fell on our feet. I unbuttoned my coat and felt like my act was in high gear. With a little luck, I'd be home in three months.

31

As soon as I got my date, I wanted to relax and hang loose until it came up.

I should've known better. The Mission was no place to coast through, especially in winter. In winter, the concrete sandwich gets tight as a new pair of shoes. It was too cold to walk the yards most evenings, so 800 of us were kept in the main building from 4 P.M. on. We could pace in the hallways, lie on our bunks, or go down to the gym for a little recreation. Or so it was called. The gym was my natural choice, but after a while I shied away from it. As facilities go, the gym wasn't much.

The only reason it was called by that name was police practice. It wasn't a gym in the way I had always used the word. The ceiling was six feet from the floor and lined with steam pipes. The room was shaped like a T with one wing for Ping-Pong, one wing for dominoes, and a third piled with weightlifting equipment. Most nights, the crowd topped out at around 250 men, and the foot of air next to the ceiling was 90 percent cigarette smoke. But that was nothing compared to the noise. The sound in the place was packed so tight it felt solid. The roar of 250 players tended to freeze me in one spot, and it never died down. The noise just hit the concrete and skittered along the pipes. I always figured it took an hour after everyone left for it to get quiet again.

Up until January, Bo Diddly put out more noise pound for pound than anybody else in the gym. Bo Diddly was a regular at the domino tables, and famous for his style. Bo always stood up to slap his domino into the game.

"Work with them fours, you cross-eyed mother-fucker," he'd shout, "and mark up fifteen more for old Bo Diddly, king of the table. Oooooweee," he'd chuckle as he sat back down, "Bo is hot tonight." Until he got transferred to the Work Release quarters outside the walls in January, Bo always slammed his domino so hard the table shook. I admired Bo's style, but he had a mixed reputation.

Old Robert said Bo was a snitch. I respected Robert, but I didn't pay much attention.

I should have. A snitch is the most dangerous thing there is.

32

A snitch is so dangerous because you can't tell him from anybody else. He walks like a convict and talks like a convict, but wears a uniform over his heart. The worst thing a snitch does is exist. Because there is such a thing, no one else is quite free to trust the man next to him. Snitches keep people with no resource except each other from reaching out and finding the company they need. Scum like that are poison in the well. There was no worse name anybody in the Mission could have been called.

Needless to say, spreading that kind of word about someone was no small matter. Lives were lost over less, and if you said it, you had better be ready to offer proof. When a prisoner heard the name applied to himself, the response tended to be stiff. In the last week of January, I watched Old Robert himself confront the label in no uncertain terms. With the aid of his box of newspaper clippings, Robert won his case.

Fast Eddie was the source of his problem. Eddie worked as a clerk in Gyro Gearloose's office and was appointed editor of the inmate newspaper. He got his job because of Gearloose's friendship, and as a result wasn't held in very high esteem by the rest of us. On Thanksgiving, he wrote an editorial advising us all to write our parents and tell them we were sorry for what we'd done. Fast Eddie also has a big mouth. Shortly after 1971 began, he started spreading a story that he'd seen Old Robert sneaking into the captain's office to give somebody up. His biggest mistake was telling Guano, one of Robert's best friends.

When Robert heard, the first thing he did was to go to the cardboard box he kept under his bunk. For the ten years he'd been locked up, Old Robert clipped newspapers and kept the results in his box. It took Robert five minutes to find the clip he wanted. Then he went looking for Eddie, with Guano and the Carrot along to help out. Guano had a knife, and Carrot had a lock knotted into the end of an old sock. If he needed to, Carrot planned to swing it around his head to use it like a mace and chain. Robert himself had a length of pipe and the newspaper clipping.

The three of them found Fast Eddie coming out the education department door into the yard by the laundry. It was 3:30 P.M., and a crowd was coming out of the clothing room with fresh underwear. The sun was covering the wall around Eddie's door. Guano and Carrot stood by the railing, and Old Robert walked straight up to Gearloose's clerk. He grabbed Fast Eddie by the front of his shirt.

"We're gonna hold court," Robert began.

"What you mean?" Eddie jabbered. "What's this court shit?" His eyes swam between Robert and his two friends.

Robert slapped him. "I mean hold court," Robert repeated. "I brought a jury to hear the case." Robert gestured toward Guano and Carrot three steps away.

Fast Eddie didn't say a thing.

After a pause to catch his breath, Old Robert began his defense.

"You been sayin some things about me, haven't you?"

"No," Fast Eddie lied, "I ain't said nothin."

"Well, what did you say to Guano there about me turnin dudes into the Heat. This man's my friend and he tells me you got stories, all kinds of stories. You gonna tell Guano here that he's a liar?"

Old Robert motioned at Guano, but Eddie wouldn't look. Robert grabbed him by the jaw and forced his head around. Then he snapped it back so hard his ear slammed against the door.

"I didn't hear you," Old Robert said. "What'd you say?"

"I'm sorry," Eddie pleaded. "I didn't mean nothin."

"You're sorry for what?"

"I'm sorry for sayin you were talkin to the police."

"You mean you told Guano there a lie?"

"I told him a lie," Fast Eddie confessed. "You never snitched nobody." Eddie looked like he was going to cry. His eyes were like egg yolks.

"I don't want no trouble," Eddie begged.

"We'll get to that when I finish the second part of my case," Old Robert said. "First, I want everybody's attention."

He already had it. The underwear crowd outside the laundry was all watching. Old Robert fished a newspaper clipping out of his pocket.

"You know," he said, "I knew your face when I first saw it. It seemed to me I remembered you from Leavenworth, so I checked my files. Tell me what this is." With his free hand, Old Robert jammed the clipping in Fast Eddie's face.

"Looks like a clipping from a paper."

"What's the headline?"

"It says 'Government Witness Turns Evidence to Committee.'"

"And whose picture is in the middle of the story?"

Fast Eddie swallowed and didn't talk until Old Robert tightened his grip on Eddie's shirt. "It's me," Eddie finally admitted. His voice had begun sloshing like dishwater.

"And what does the caption under the picture say?"

Fast Eddie wouldn't answer.

Old Robert slammed his head into the door, and Eddie changed his mind.

"It says, 'Edward Barnes . . .'"

"Louder," Robert interrupted.

Eddie cleared his throat. "It says, 'Edward Barnes, star witness, testifies before committee.'" The words hung on Eddie's lips then dribbled down his chin.

"So what does that make you?"

"A snitch."

"Say it louder," Robert continued, "so everybody can hear you."

"A SNITCH."

"A little louder. We got a man on the jury who's half deaf."

"A SNITCH." Fast Eddie said it loud enough to be heard inside the laundry.

"Now I'm gonna give you your sentence," Robert concluded. "Since you plead guilty, I ain't gonna hurt you this time. But if I ever hear you even mention my name again, you're gonna get paroled in a box."

Fast Eddie shivered. After a moment's silence, Robert dropped Eddie's shirt and walked back across the yard. It was almost time for count.

Guano slapped Fast Eddie before he left. "Don't tell no more lies," he warned.

As far as I know, Eddie didn't. From then on, Fast Eddie seemed to keep to himself.

33

The next worse thing to a snitch is a fool. A fool can cause almost as much trouble, and not even know he's doing it. A week after Old Robert cleared his name, my friend Deuce McGuire stumbled over one of those, and it cost him dearly. The fool's name was Dagwood.

Dagwood's old lady came up from Tucson to visit on Sunday. She had some stuff and some pills to give him, but she forgot to bring a balloon to smuggle it in. Like the fool he was, Dagwood had his cellie drop one onto the visiting yard from the honor block window. Dagwood should have been busted dead to rights, but the Greaseball had his back turned, messing with the vending machine, and didn't see a thing.

Dagwood managed to get through shakedown without a mistake, but only barely. As soon as he passed the Control Room, he stuck his finger in his throat and headed for the yard. Out there, he and his cellie stood around while Dagwood tried to puke. That took ten minutes and attracted considerable attention, but never reached the police. Dagwood finally succeeded, and brought up the dope in a lurch of lunch meat and brown pulp. Dagwood bent over, fished the balloon out of the puddle, and took off with his cellie for the honor block. Dagwood stuck the balloon in his shorts and they both looked over their shoulders a lot.

This fool, Dagwood, was a lucky son of a bitch, and spent the next hour pushing his luck to the limits. He and his cellie meant to shoot up right away, but before they could fetch their outfit from the mattress, Jungle Jim walked in. By all rights that should have been a bust. Dagwood had the balloon in his shirt pocket, and Jungle Jim was a famous shakedown artist. Jim smiled.

But that was all. He moved on down the hall, and the fool and his cellie listened as the outside door opened and shut when the cop left. Five minutes later, they were both off and nodding. Everything from there on in would have gone fine if the fool had just kept to himself, but Dagwood was too dumb for that. He and his cellie split for the hall, loaded like freight cars.

There was a lot of traffic out there on a Sunday night, and Dagwood took a position in the middle of the action, leaned back on the concrete wall, and nodded like a yo-yo. It would have been subtler to put a sign that said "stoned" around his neck. In ten minutes, fifteen beggars were lined up on either side, asking for a taste.

Jefferson Davis was the first beggar in line. Jefferson was fat as a bathtub and had an extra sense just for dope.

"Come on, homey," he chided Dagwood, "just a little taste for old Jeff. I ain't gonna tell nobody."

Dagwood felt generous, so he took Jeff down to the shitters in One West and got him off. Afterward, the fool decided to do Deuce a favor in the same spirit. He and Deuce worked together in the electric shop. He found McGuire on his bunk in Four East where he and I were playing hearts against Hopalong Cassidy and the Baldwin City Kid. Dagwood walked up with his cellie and stopped at the locker across the row from Deuce McGuire's bunk.

"Hey, Deuce," Dagwood hissed. "Come over here."

Deuce put his hand down and walked over.

"I got a little present," the fool explained.

Deuce looked around for the cop, but Dagwood reassured him. "Don't worry," the fool said, "my cellie'll stand point."

That was the way etiquette demanded such deals be done, but Deuce shouldn't have counted on Dagwood's cellie. He was something of a fool himself, and was loaded to the gills. The cop was down by the TV when the cellie turned around to watch Deuce and Dagwood. The cop turned at the same time and saw Dagwood hand Deuce two pills. The cop came running and pounced on McGuire when he got back to the bunk. His first reach was around the handful of pills.

"What you got there?" the law said.

Deuce responded in a flash. He hit the cop across the face with his free hand and swallowed the dope. The cop jumped away and ran after Dagwood. The fool had just figured out what was happening, and turned to run.

"Flush em down the shitter," his cellie shouted.

The fool had a head start, but he was too fucked up to make it there. He wandered out into the hall with a blank look instead. The cop caught up and kept right on going, hand in hand with Dagwood, until they reached the lieutenant's office.

"Empty your pockets," the lieutenant said.

The fool did. Out came the balloon looking like twenty years.

It should have been, but the fool's luck held. Dagwood went to the Basement for a week and then got sent to Terminal Island. Deuce McGuire did a month locked up for hitting the cop.

After it happened, Old Robert asked me to see if I could smuggle some cigarettes down to Deuce's cell. I said I'd try.

"Shit," Old Robert added, "it gets like this every winter. Every place I been, it's always the same way. The shit gets stirred up and don't settle until spring." We were walking along the upstairs hall, turned when we reached the door to Two East, and headed back the way we'd come.

"You're lucky, Harris," Robert said on our way back in the other direction. "You don't got to do any more winters after this one. Shit, man, you're short."

I grinned like I was embarrassed. "Sure am," I smiled. "Knock on wood."

I looked for a place to do it, but there wasn't a scrap of wood to be seen. I settled for a plastic bucket in the mop closet, but it wasn't the same.

34

Three quarters of the way through February, my luck seemed to run out. I got caught in a cross fire set up by Joe Friday and Bo Diddly, Friday's pet snake. It was a sucker play and I fell for it. The mistake came within an inch of costing my date, and a lot more besides that.

It happened on a Tuesday. The sun was squeezing through the clouds in occasional chunks. For the last month, I'd been working with the landscape crew in the village of hacks living outside the walls. Except for a few, the only convicts out there went back inside at three. The exceptions were held in the Work Release quarters building at hacktown's back edge. These men were all six months short, and were allowed to go out to the streets and hold down a job during the day. Bo Diddly was the only long one out there. He had two years left. That in itself should have tipped me off, but my head was already halfway to California. Bo worked as the driver, ferrying convicts into El Paso in the morning and back at night. I was given a pair of clippers in the morning and told to move down the road, trimming bushes.

By two, I'd reached Work Release, and decided to take a break. I went into the quarters' kitchen and poured myself a cup of coffee. I sat on the back steps drinking it until I heard the screen door creak open. Bo was standing behind me.

"Hey, Harris," he said, "come on in my room. I got a little somethin for ya."

I thought about it a second, and then gave in to temptation. It'd been a while since I'd had anything to mellow out in back of. I followed Bo Diddly down the narrow hallway to his room, and closed the door.

Bo reached under his mattress and pulled out a sack of weed. I sat on one end of the bunk while Bo pulled up a chair. Diddly rolled a number and handed it across the blanket to me. I lit the herb and took a deep hit, letting the smoke curl across my lip and up my nose. Bo and I finished in three minutes. When we were done, the edges of my world were full of light. I thanked him and stood up.

"I appreciate it," I said. "It's been a while."

"Man, don't run off," Bo whined. "Visit with me for a while."

"I got to get back on those hedges, Bo," I explained. "My boss'll get all over my ass."

"Well, take one to smoke inside," he said. Bo didn't wait for me to answer, and rolled another joint real quick. He reached over and dropped it in my jacket pocket.

"Stay high," he said.

I closed the door behind me, made my way out with a stop on the back porch for my clippers, and headed around the building to get at the bushes. One step past the corner, I did a quick about-face and jumped back behind the quarters' wall. Joe Friday was waiting in front of the building in a pickup truck. He had a hack named Walrus with him. I reached in my pocket for Bo's joint and flipped it into the flower bed. Then I stepped back out and began trimming the hedge that ran along the sunny side of the building. Joe Friday saw me this time, and jumped out of the cab.

"Harris," he yelled, "get over here."

I walked across the lawn. "What's up?" I said when I got close.

"Shakedown," Friday growled.

He didn't have to tell me how to do it. I was familiar with the technique. I reached into my pockets, took everything out in my hands, and lifted them over my head. When I was standing there like that, the Walrus stepped up and knocked me on my ass. It was a right cross that he used. I hit the ground with my pockets spread out for ten feet in either direction.

"What's that bullshit about?" I asked from my back.

"Shut up and wait for the captain to get here," Friday answered. Walrus was headed for the truck to call in on the radio.

I lay in the dust and felt the cross hairs zero in on me. Over and over in my head I kept saying, "But I've got less than thirty days." No one seemed to pay much attention. I was nervous as hell, and started to ask a question after the Walrus returned from calling the captain.

"Shut up," Friday cut me off.

I did. We sat in silence for five minutes until John Wayne drove up with two other hacks. The Walrus took the two others and me into a room inside the quarters, and told me to strip. When I got naked, they had me bend over and spread my cheeks. I passed the inspection with a breeze, and got my clothes back on.

Joe Friday and John Wayne walked in when I finished buttoning my shirt. Joe Friday stopped in front of me with Bo Diddly's joint in his hand.

"This is yours," he said.

"Bullshit."

"We found it in your goddamn pocket when we shook you down." Friday's voice was a straight line.

"It ain't mine," I maintained. "I never seen that thing."

"You got it from someone out here, didn't you?"

"I don't know what you're talkin about," I swore. "I don't have nothin to do with that shit in your hand."

John Wayne cut the interrogation off. "Get in the truck," he said. I followed instructions, and sat in the bed of the pickup with a cop on either side. John Wayne drove through the back gate and stopped at the edge of the yard. One of the cops took me to the Basement while John Wayne found the associate warden. Joe Friday went with him. The last I ever saw of Friday was his back hunching away and leaning toward the captain with the taste of blood on his tongue.

35

The taste on my tongue was cotton. I can't recall ever being scared more. My insides frosted over, my feet got heavy, and my mind moved down into my spine. I sat down on my bunk in the Basement, 100 percent wired. Without a thought in my brain. All my thinking was out in my fingers, in my toes, and dripping down my neck. I imagined I was a tomcat cornered by hounds. John Wayne came by in an hour and said to follow him. It was a short walk to the associate warden's office.

The A.W. was behind his desk. He sat straight, as if someone had left a filing cabinet in the chair. John Wayne sat along the wall next to Errol Flynn. I sat out in the middle of the floor, and stared at the venetian blind. When the A.W. shuffled the papers on his desk, I looked at the mole on his cheek. It had three two-inch hairs growing out of it.

"We have reason to believe," he began, "that you were in possession of marijuana on a federal reservation, a crime punishable by ten years in prison." The mole shimmied as he spoke.

"What gives you reason to believe that?" I challenged.

The A.W. cleared his throat. "Officer Friday has filed a disciplinary report to that effect," he explained.

"It's bullshit," I argued. "That dog's been trying to make a case on me since I walked in the door." The words were squeezing between my teeth. The fear had given me lockjaw.

"Watch your mouth," John Wayne warned.

"Forget my mouth," I snapped back, "it's my ass I'm worried about." I figured to break down some of the tension with a little humor. It worked fine for me, but left the rest of the room basically untouched. Flynn smirked, but that was all.

The A.W. leaned back in his chair. "With good reason," he added, "we're referring the case to the federal attorney. Until he decides to prosecute or not, you'll be kept in lockup."

"You can't be serious," I said.

They were. John Wayne called the Evil Stepmother on the phone and told him to come get me. The two of us walked back to the Basement. I stepped inside the gate and he released the lever in the control box down by the door. My gate slid shut with a thump that sounded much too final for my liking. I wanted to call the Stepmother and ask him not to leave me alone. The fear was inside my cage. I could feel it stalking me, and I wasn't looking forward to the fight.

36

I went one to one with my fear for the next two weeks. The first night I didn't sleep at all. When I finally dozed off, I woke up in an hour and found I'd soaked the blanket with sweat.

I eventually fought my fear to a draw, but I have to admit I got burned in the process. To deal with the ten years hanging over my head, I had to kill my short and lose a little of myself in the process.

I'd been growing toward the streets over the last two months. Ever since I got my date, I'd been opening up and looking over the walls. I'd begun thinking of myself as someplace besides where I was. I was easing into life outside, and trying to prepare myself. Joe Friday ended all that. I couldn't afford that kind of thinking anymore. Hoping only plays into fear's hands. In self-defense, I reached for my ax and chopped off the me that was growing toward the door. It drifted away, and I didn't watch it go. I had other things to do.

I had to come to terms with myself. I had to recover from the shock and get lucky quick. My life was in the balance. I walked back and forth a lot and drew the number ten on the floor with the heel of my shoe. The Wasp saw the marking and kidded me about it.

"Don't worry, man," he advised. "They ain't got no penitentiary case on you. Just sit tight and hold yer mud, it'll all work out." I got to be up front with the Wasp, because the back was already full. John Wayne had busted Queen Bee and six others in the Catholic chapel the week before. He hadn't told them why yet, but it appeared to be part of his semiannual crackdown on blow jobs.

I wanted to believe the Wasp but I didn't. I felt like I had an anchor tied to my leg. I didn't believe it until Errol Flynn told me himself the next week. The Stepmother opened my cell and walked me to the parole office. The sun outside the window was thick as buttermilk. Flynn told me the federal attorney didn't want to touch the case. "You'll be out of lockup after the four o'clock count," he said.

"And go home next week," Flynn added. "If you think you can hold tight that long." He grinned.

I tried to, but for the moment, I'd forgotten just how to do it.

At 4:40, I moved myself back to Number 24 up in the Birdcage. Curly was still living on the top bunk, but he was out for exercise. While I'd been gone, the night shift hack had torn all my pictures off the wall and taken all my library books back to the shelves. My painting kit had been confiscated and my box of letters searched.

It still felt like home. I stayed there long enough to look around, and then headed for the yard.

I walked past the hospital and down the staircase. When I reached the main corridor, I heard yelling from down the hall. Officer Fuck was coming my way at full steam. "Out of the way," he huffed, "outta my way." He had a body over his shoulder.

The body's name was Moon. He was a junky from Laredo. Fuck found him in the honor block with a lifetime's worth of heroin in his veins. Moon was already dead, but Fuck didn't know it yet. He was just concentrating on getting to the hospital.

When the cop and the body got as far as me, Moon's head was bobbing with the roll of fat Fuck's chest. Moon's eyes were bugged out, and his cheeks turning blue.

"Outta my way," Fuck yelled.

I watched him go by and up the stairs. Moon's face stuck in my mind. I could see it bobbing under the cop's shoulder and between his own dead legs. It stared at me upside down.

When I got out in the yard, I could hear the whap of handballs off the wall, but all I could see was Moon's face. It stared at me upside down.

"I gotta get out of this motherfucker," I said to myself. "Soon."

37

I got my wish, but not before the birds in the Basement threw a good-by party. I couldn't be there to join in, but I listened to it all.

I spent my last day inside the Mission on my bunk. I didn't want to see the hall or the yard. I lay up, and listened to the birds instead. Curly even talked to them on the telephone.

The telephone was commonly known as a sewer pipe, but it can be adapted to a number of different purposes. Curly covered the top of the shitter, and pumped it until all the water was forced out of the bowl. When Queen Bee did the same thing on the floor below, they could both stick their heads down in the toilet and talk to each other. She kept us informed of the progress they were making. Queen Bee and the birds started things off by taking a book of smuggled matches and burning a mattress. The stench and smoke blew out into the hall and brought John Wayne in short order. He had the riot squad with him and killed the blaze with a fire hose. Then the cops took all the mattresses and told the birds they'd have to sleep on steel. When the captain and his friends left, Queen Bee rang us up. She said they hadn't seen shit yet.

And she kept her word. After she hung up, Queen Bee tore the leg off her bunk and started busting crockery. She beat the sink into rubble and finished the shitter the same way. Using the end of her steel stump, she beat a hole into the water pipe, and it began flooding the Basement. The water ran down to the Evil Step-mother's post in five minutes, and passed out into the main hallway. The Stepmother ran for John Wayne's office. While he was gone, Queen Bee shouted that we should flush some cigarettes. Curly did like she asked, and sent a pack of Camels down the pipe. Queen Bee reached through the hole she'd carved and snatched them as they came by. When John Wayne showed up, Queen Bee was lying back on her bunk, blowing smoke rings. The captain cuffed her hands and legs and laid her on the floor in an inch of water. She stayed that way the rest of the night. The party was over.

Queen Bee's friend, Laurace Scudder, rattled her cell door all night in protest. I listened to the regular thump for a long time after lights out. I had no real expectations of sleep. I was trying to see what was about to happen to me, but it wasn't all that clear. Curly was laid out on the top tier, and I tried to explain it to him.

"I'm beginning to think people really do get out of here," I said.

Curly was asleep, and just kicked his feet.

Not that it mattered. I didn't really want an answer. The only thing I really wanted was morning. When I finally fell asleep, Laurace's banging door sounded like the workings of some giant clock.

38

At 7:30, the Evil Stepmother took me down to the clothing room to dress out. I put on a gray suit and a pink shirt, and headed for the streets. The Carrot was waiting by the Control Room to say good-by. He slapped my hand.

"You so short you smokin," he laughed. "Whatcha gonna do first?"

"Buy an *Evergreen Review*," I joked.

Carrot laughed, and walked a few steps with me. I didn't slow down. He stopped at the caseworker's office, and I kept walking. I felt like a coiled spring.

"Save the back issues," he shouted after me.

I heard him, but didn't look back. I was looking ahead to that last gate. Joanie and the kid were waiting on the other side. She hugged me when I reached her, and we walked out on the Mission's porch. Across the way, the sun was slopping along one edge of the tower. The round head swiveled in his seat to look at us.

"Let's go home," I said.

39

I tried to.

Swear to God, we both did. When they let me out, home was where I was told to go, but I couldn't find it. I looked and looked, but I must have put it down in one of those long hallways and forgot where I'd left it. Maybe Joanie packed it and forgot which trunk. Wherever it was, it was someplace else. I went to my old lady's house like I was falling in a well. There weren't any cops there, but the ones who weren't were stuck to my brain like plaster. I was used to living in a bear trap, and had a hard time believing I was anyplace else. There were miles between us. She said I was crazy, and I suppose in her own way she was right.

I wasn't righteously crazy, but I wasn't all that adjusted either. The only thing I trusted was the me I'd spent the last twenty months with. The only place I knew to be in was the place inside myself where I'd been living for such a long time. There were just more door knobs to turn and long corridors to escape from than I was up to in her company. She was rich and I loved her, but that didn't seem to help. When it came time to leave, there weren't a lot of good-bys to be said. I just found the door and used it. When I did, I didn't feel like I was doing something I hadn't done before.

Sometimes I drive down to J.C.'s farm in Raisin City, and we talk about the time behind us. It's been a while since I was locked up and it doesn't haunt me anymore, but I haven't forgotten much.

And I haven't tried very hard either. Forgetting's just not what I have in mind.

"Only a fool can't remember the name of the dog that bit him," is what J.C. says.